Social Network Analysis and Egyptology

This book addresses Social Network Analysis (SNA) as a methodological approach in the field of Egyptology, exploring its possibilities, limitations, and applications within the discipline.

Social Network Analysis is a sociological, graph theory–based approach used to investigate social structures created by patterns of relationships (ties or links) between actors (nodes), which has been utilised by scholars in other areas of ancient history. The book first provides readers with basic information on the theoretical background of methods applied in SNA, as well as network theory and Actor-Network Theory (ANT) more generally. It discusses the history of SNA specifically within the discipline of Egyptology, evaluating the advantages and limitations of this approach when applied to different types of datasets, such as written sources and material records. The author then explores a case study, examining the potential of network modelling on datasets from the Abydos votive zone during the Middle Kingdom period (c. 2040–1750 BC). The book highlights how SNA and network theory can be useful supplementary tools alongside more traditional research approaches in Egyptology for a more comprehensive understanding of social relations and interconnections in ancient contexts.

Social Network Analysis and Egyptology is suitable for students and scholars working on Egyptology who are interested in SNA methodology, as well as those working on Classical and Ancient Near Eastern archaeology and history. It also appeals to those interested in network research and theory more broadly. Colour versions of images in this book can be found in the Support Material: www.routledge.com/9781032599632.

Danijela Stefanović is an ancient historian and Egyptologist. She is a tenured professor of Ancient Greek and Near Eastern History at the University of Belgrade (Faculty of Philosophy). The main focus of her research is prosopography and the social history of Ancient Egypt during the II millennium BC.

Routledge Focus on Egyptology

Recent titles include:

From Mummies to Microchips
A Case-Study in Effective Online Teaching Developed at the University of Manchester
Joyce Tyldesley and Nicky Nielsen

Social Network Analysis and Egyptology
Danijela Stefanović

Social Network Analysis and Egyptology

Danijela Stefanović

Routledge
Taylor & Francis Group
LONDON AND NEW YORK

First published 2024
by Routledge
4 Park Square, Milton Park, Abingdon, Oxon OX14 4RN

and by Routledge
605 Third Avenue, New York, NY 10158

Routledge is an imprint of the Taylor & Francis Group, an informa business

© 2024 Danijela Stefanović

The right of Danijela Stefanović to be identified as author of this work has been asserted in accordance with sections 77 and 78 of the Copyright, Designs and Patents Act 1988.

All rights reserved. No part of this book may be reprinted or reproduced or utilised in any form or by any electronic, mechanical, or other means, now known or hereafter invented, including photocopying and recording, or in any information storage or retrieval system, without permission in writing from the publishers.

Trademark notice: Product or corporate names may be trademarks or registered trademarks, and are used only for identification and explanation without intent to infringe.

British Library Cataloguing-in-Publication Data
A catalogue record for this book is available from the British Library

Library of Congress Cataloging-in-Publication Data
Names: Stefanović, Danijela, author.
Title: Social network analysis and Egyptology/Danijela Stefanović.
Description: Abingdon, Oxon; New York, NY: Routledge, 2024. |
Series: Routledge focus on Egyptology |
Includes bibliographical references and index.
Identifiers: LCCN 2023051189 (print) | LCCN 2023051190 (ebook) |
ISBN 9781032599632 (hardback) | ISBN 9781032599649 (paperback) |
ISBN 9781003457015 (ebook)
Subjects: LCSH: Egyptology–Methodology. | Egypt–Social life and customs–To 332 B.C. | Social networks–Egypt–History–To 1500. | Social sciences–Network analysis. | Social sciences and history.
Classification: LCC DT61 .S8665 2024 (print) | LCC DT61 (ebook) |
DDC 932–dc23/eng/20231208
LC record available at https://lccn.loc.gov/2023051189
LC ebook record available at https://lccn.loc.gov/2023051190

ISBN: 978-1-032-59963-2 (hbk)
ISBN: 978-1-032-59964-9 (pbk)
ISBN: 978-1-003-45701-5 (ebk)

DOI: 10.4324/9781003457015

Typeset in Times New Roman
by Deanta Global Publishing Services, Chennai, India

Access the Support Material: www.routledge.com/9781032599632

Contents

List of Figures *vi*

1 Introduction 1

2 Social Network Analysis – a brief overview 8

3 A long-short way from Ruffini's *Social Networks in Byzantine Egypt* 20
 3.1 Trismegistos 26

4 Social Network Analysis and Egyptology – should I stay, or should I go? 33

5 'The small world of the Abydos votive zone' – the game of graphs, glyphs, and objects 50
 5.1 Setting a scene 50
 5.2 The treasurer Ikhernefret and ANOC 1 55
 5.3 The curious case of the lady rn(.j)-n.j and ANOC XXII 58
 5.4 Micro ego-networks as parts of the macro networks of treasurers Senbsumai and Senebi 61
 5.5 The 'small world' of the Abydos votive zone – the game of graphs, glyphs, and objects 69

6 Some final remarks for future research 90

 Index *95*

Figures

2.1	Betweenness centrality of nodes in a directed graph	12
4.1	The one-mode network of the 'soldier' ('ḫ³wtj) Sneferu	36
4.2	The one-mode network of the lady t³-ntt-n.j	39
4.3	Two-mode network of the list of workers preserved on the verso of the late Middle Kingdom papyrus Brooklyn 35.1446 and additional documents	41
4.4	One-mode network of the list of workers preserved on the verso of the late Middle Kingdom papyrus Brooklyn 35.1446	42
5.1	The one-mode network of ANOC 1	57
5.2	The ego-network of the treasurer Ikhernefret	58
5.3	The two-mode macro network of Ikhernefret	59
5.4	The one-mode macro network of Ikhernefret	60
5.5	The two-mode network of the lady rn(.j)-n.j	62
5.6	The one-mode network of the lady rn(.j)-n.j	63
5.7	The one-mode network of the lady jw-bnrj (III)	64
5.8	The two-mode network of the lady jw-bnrj (III)	65
5.9	The one-mode network of the group of officials operating before the treasurer Senebi	66
5.10	The two-mode network of the group of officials operating before the treasurer Senebi	67
5.11	Simplified one-mode network of the treasurer Senebi	68
5.12	One-mode network of the ANOC 7, 19 and 32	74
5.13	Two-mode network of ANOCs 7, 19, and 32	75
5.14	The one-mode network of the ten ANOC clusters with 363 individuals and 9,372 links	76
5.15	The two-mode network of the ten ANOC clusters	77

1 Introduction

> Humanistic data are almost by definition uncertain, open to interpretation, flexible, and not easily definable. ... Humanists face problems from the outset: data that do not fit neatly into one category or the other, complex situations that ought not be reduced, and methods that were developed with different purposes in mind. However, network analysis remains a viable methodology for answering and raising humanistic questions – we simply must be cautious and must be willing to get our hands dirty editing the algorithms to suit our needs.
>
> (Weingart, 2011)

Gradual development and important progress in network and graph theories, from the mid-XX century on, offered many new perspectives for various research fields. Relying on the multitude of mathematical, social, economic, cultural, and relational concepts for the structural analysis of human relations and interactions, the network approach and its multiple sub-branches (including Social Network Analysis) have slowly but steadily knocked at the door of Humanities.

Social Network Analysis (SNA) is a graph theory–based approach, created to explore social structures through the use of networks.[1] Relying on the network approach theory, which refers to the study of systems and patterns recognised in network graphs, Social Network Analysis aims to detect and measure various types of relatedness within a given group or community.

The network approach has been applied to a wide range of archaeological and historical datasets and contexts in various ways and with variable outcomes. Consequently, within the last few decades, network analysis has increasingly featured in the Classical and Ancient Near Eastern Studies.

Within the field of history, the first study that focused on the reconstruction of the model of relatedness appeared in 1979. Richard M. Smith published in the *Journal of Family History* the paper of a very conspicuous title: 'Kin and Neighbors in a Thirteenth-Century Suffolk Community.'[2] Smith analysed the 13,592 interactions of 575 individuals of a village in medieval England,

2 *Introduction*

between 1259 and 1293, detecting the 'ego-zones' of some prominent persons and providing the 'calculation of the network density.' However, his innovative approach was to remain isolated for more than 20 years.

John F. Padgett and Christopher Ansell published in 1993, in the *American Journal of Sociology*, a paper entitled 'Robust Action and the Rise of the Medici 1400–1434.'[3] The rich corpus of data allowed for the analysis of different types of networks (marriage, economic, political, and clientelistic) of 92 elite families in 1400s Florence. Padgett and Ansell demonstrated, with the application of network models, how members of the Medici family controlled and shaped various aspects of the community's life. Their study widely opened the door to the network approach within history (and archaeology).

In 1990, Michael Alexander and James Danowski published the paper 'Analysis of an Ancient Network: Personal Communication and the Study of Social Structure in a Past Society,'[4] performing a Social Network Analysis on Cicero's letters between 68 and 50 BC. This was the first study to combine network theory and historical texts in the field of ancient history. Although the presented results may not have been as successful as Alexander and Danowski had hoped, their research demonstrated that a historical network approach was possible for ancient sources.

However, after Alexander and Danowski's work, the field of Classical Studies remained silent for almost 20 years. In 2006, Shawn Graham made an important contribution to the field. He studied 234 named Roman brick manufacturers known to us from stamps, dating from the first through the third centuries AD, who formed a network based on family ties, industrial relationships, or co-location. Graham was able to reconstruct relationships between workshops and situate them along the Tiber River.[5] His research opened a new chapter in the field of Classical Studies.

Two years later, Giovanni Ruffini published *Social Networks in Byzantine Egypt*.[6] Ruffini's study presented a prosopographic overview of Oxyrhynchos and Aphrodito, as well as a network analysis of data from these two locations. This important and challenging study on the social history of late antiquity exemplifies the potential of the network approach in the field of ancient history.

The first decades of the XXI century witnessed a vast flourishing of network approaches in history and archaeology, including in Classical and Ancient Near Eastern Studies, as it became more common for scholars of the ancient world to consider network modelling. Researchers have focused on issues of kinship, local communities, friendship, political ties and conflicts, commodities distribution, production centres, geographical patterns of trade, migration, and religious beliefs. Unfortunately, Egyptology remains a latecomer.

A new generation of scholars interested in the network approach has been also very active through several research groups. The interdisciplinary *Connected Past* group,[7] forcefully advocating for the network approach, has held several workshops and conferences since 2011. In 2016 the group members published a volume entitled *The Connected Past: Challenges to Network Studies in Archaeology and History*, edited by Tom Brughmans, Anna Collar, and Fiona Coward – some of the most influential scholars in the field. Collar's *Religious Networks in the Roman Empire* demonstrated how the application of network theory to the study of religion in the Roman Empire can enhance our understanding of the spread of new cults and cultic practices.[8]

The group *Réseaux et Histoire* ('*Networks and History*'), RES-HIST, established by Claire Lemercier, "aims at fostering discussions among historians interested in networks and at promoting the use of concepts and methods borrowed from other disciplines, but adapted to ours."[9]

The web platform of the *Historical Network Research Community* (HNR)[10] is an important research tool for scholars interested in network analysis. Its history goes back to the year 2009, when Ulrich Eumann, Martin Stark, Linda von Keyserlingk-Rehbein, and Marten Düring decided to organise a workshop for historians interested in Social Network Analysis. Over the years, the HNR community has grown to become an internationally oriented group of scholars from different academic disciplines who are linked by their shared interests in the analysis of historical networks. The HNR organises workshops, conferences, and lectures, maintains an open access journal, and produces a research bibliography.

Although HNR's *Journal of Historical Network Research*[11] is interdisciplinary and oriented towards the publication of original contributions applying the theories and methodologies of (social) network analysis to historical research, the fourth volume was dedicated to the theories and methodologies of Social Network Analysis of Greco-Roman politics.[12] The editors stated that the publication was the first attempt in English to introduce the advantages of network analysis, with a stress on recent and ongoing network research, to a wider audience of classicists and ancient historians.

An important tool for obtaining an overview of the works focusing on the network analysis of ancient and near eastern sources is the *Historical Network Research Bibliography*.[13]

Near Eastern Studies followed researchers from the world of Classical Studies. In 2014, Caroline Waerzeggers introduced the main concepts, methods, and perspectives of Social Network Analysis to Assyriology. In her study of Babylonia in the I millennium BC, she used network theories to analyse cuneiform tablets, but also addressed the question of whether SNA could offer promising and useful perspectives in the field of Assyriology.[14] This book addresses the same question regarding Egyptology.

The great advantage of the cuneiform corpora is that many of the existing cuneiform texts are presented in a digital form that allows Assyriologists, and other Near Eastern scholars, to apply the network approach to datasets.[15] The network approach has been applied to the analysis of individual archives,[16]

4 *Introduction*

studies on society,[17] religion,[18] and the Akkadian lexica.[19] The Old Assyrian letter corpus (c. 1950–1750 BC) from Kaneš – that is, the network of Assyrian merchants in Kaneš and Aššur – has also been successfully studied using a network approach.[20]

Émilie Pagé-Perron, in her paper 'Network Analysis for Reproducible Research on Large Administrative Cuneiform Corpora,' addresses the prospects of SNA in research on large datasets, presenting a case study of 2,700 administrative documents from Late Early Dynastic and Old Akkadian Adab (a site in southern Iraq, c. 2400–2200 BC).[21] The chosen corpus contained 800 individuals (i.e., personal names) connected by 7,000 relations. Pagé-Perron pointed out that "quantitative approaches also offer new means to systematically store information in a manner that retains factors that are not already known to be meaningful."[22]

Instead of providing a reader with a complete and profound overview of scholarly achievements of network studies in the fields of Classical and Ancient Near Eastern Studies, the author intends to hint at where, for example, Assyriology is heading, and why Egyptology is not mentioned at all. The topic of Social Network Analysis and Egyptology will be discussed in detail in the forthcoming pages.

Social Network Analysis and Egyptology is neither a manual nor a how-to-do book. If we step aside from the general theoretical context of network theory, it would be hard (perhaps even impossible!) to provide a universal tool: for each individual research project, the addressed question or research goal, methods, parameters, measurements, and algorithms need to be specified, modified, or created anew. The same is true for the chosen software package.

The present book will provide the reader with basic information on the theoretical background and the methods applied by Social Network Analysis, as well as on network theory and Actor-Network Theory (ANT) in a more general sense (Chapter 2). There are many useful and practical studies for gaining knowledge about network theory and its implementation on history datasets. The latest is *The Network Science in Archaeology* by T. Brughmans and M. A. Peeples.[23]

An overview of the history of Social Network Analysis within the field of Egyptology follows (Chapter 3). Compared with other branches of Classical and Near Eastern Studies, Egyptology as a discipline is still rigid toward the network analysis approach. The book will evaluate objective obstacles that prevent researchers from implanting SNA methodology (such as limited availability of the sources), but also highlight some of its advantages, especially when used as a supplementary tool to more traditional approaches (Ch. 4). Finally, based on several mini case studies (Ch.5), the author exemplifies the potential of network modelling on datasets from the period of the Middle Kingdom (c. 2040–1750 BC).

The title of Chapter 5, 'The "small world" of the Abydos votive zone – the game of graphs, glyphs, and objects,' may, perhaps, be confusing for the reader. However, there is a reason for this. The word 'game' is used here as a metaphor – a game implies rules, but with an uncertain ending. This is exactly what we are doing when implementing SNA – we are feeding software with data (either from written sources – in our case glyphs, i.e. hieroglyphs – or archaeological data), applying strict rules (various metrics and algorithms), and achieving the result with all uncertainties – the graph, or visualised snapshot of the researched topic.

The data needed for graph analysis and network modelling were collected from the author's own database (presently in the form of a FileMaker file with 32,116 individual entries), and from the online database *Persons and Names of the Middle Kingdom* (PNM).[24] All graphs were generated using Gephi software.[25]

Notes

1 For an overview of the history of SNA initially focused on human relations, see, e.g., Freeman (2004); Freeman (2011); Scott (2012), 7–30.
2 Smith (1979).
3 Padgett and Ansell (1993).
4 Alexander and Danowski (1990).
5 Graham (2006).
6 Ruffini (2008).
7 https://connectedpast.net/ (accessed August 12, 2023).
8 Collar (2013).
9 http://reshist.hypotheses.org/ (accessed August 12, 2023).
10 https://historicalnetworkresearch.org/about/ (accessed August 12, 2023).
11 http://historicalnetworkresearch.org/ (accessed August 12, 2023).
12 Broekaert et al. (2020); see also Stefanović (2020).
13 http://historicalnetworkresearch.org/resources/bibliography/ (accessed August 12, 2023).
14 Waerzeggers (2014). For the detailed discussion of the state of arts in Social Network Analysis in Assyriology see Goddeeris (2022), 370–382.
15 Digitisation projects include the *Cuneiform Digital Library Initiative* (CDLI), the *Open Richly Annotated Cuneiform Corpus* (ORACC), and *Database of Neo-Sumerian Texts* (BDTNS, after the Spanish acronym). Others have taken the approach of providing digital text editions, such as *Achemenet*. Digital text editions are texts that are provided online, but without the back-end data. Other important digital projects include: *Prosobab* and the *Geomapping Landscapes of Writing* (GLoW).
16 For example: Wagner et al. (2013); Waerzeggers (2014); King and Pirngruber (2022); Kulikov et al. (2021).
17 For the marriage practices of the priestly families in Borsippa during the Neo-Babylonian and early Persian rule (c. 620–484 BC) see Still (2019), 27–63. The Neo-Assyrian elite networks have been recently analysed by Jones (2021).
18 1,532 non-lexical texts from the Neo-Assyrian period (from the late X to the late VII centuries BC), which contain the name of Aššur and the name of another god. Alstola et al. (2019).
19 Svärd et al. (2018) and (2020); Bennett (2023).
20 Anderson (2018) and (2020).
21 Pagé-Perron (2018).

6 Introduction

22 Pagé-Perron (2018), 217.
23 Brughmans and Peeples (2023).
24 Persons and Names of the Middle Kingdom, Version 4 (accessed August 3, 2023) https://pnm.uni-mainz.de/info.
25 Bastian et al. (2009); see also Scott (2012), 103–110.

References

Alexander, M., & Danowski, J. (1990). Analysis of an ancient network: Personal communication and the study of social structure in a past society. *Social Networks, 12*(4), 313–335. https://doi.org/10.1016/0378-8733(90)90013-Y

Alstola, T., Zaia, S., Sahala, A., Jauhiainen, H., Svärd, S., & Lindén, K. (2019). Aššur and his friends: A statistical analysis of Neo-Assyrian texts. *Journal for Cuneiform Studies, 71*, 159–180. https://doi.org/10.1086/703859

Anderson, A. G. (2018). *The Old Assyrian social network: An analysis of the texts from Kültepe Kanesh (1950–1750 B.C.E.)* [Unpublished doctoral dissertation]. Harvard University. https://doi.org/10.13140/RG.2.2.29787.92967 [Stable URL: https://www.researchgate.net/publication/335703724_The_Old_Assyrian_Social_Network_an_analysis_of_the_text_from_KultepeKanesh_1950-1750_BCE]

Anderson, A. G. (2020). Death of an Old Assyrian salesman. *Chatreššar: International Journal for Indo-European, Semitic, and Cuneiform Languages, 1*, 5–34. http://hdl.handle.net/20.500.11956/123610

Bastian, M., Heymann, S., & Jacomy, M. (2009). Gephi: An open source software for exploring and manipulating networks. *Proceedings of the International AAAI Conference on Web and Social Media, 3*(1), 361–362. https://doi.org/10.1609/icwsm.v3i1.13937

Bennett, E. (2023). Age and masculinities during the Neo-Assyrian period. *Journal of Cuneiform Studies, 75*, 123–154. https://doi.org/10.1086/725222

Broekaert, W., Köstner, E., & Rollinger, C. (Eds.). (2020). The ties that bind. Ancient politics and network research. *Journal of Historical Network Research, 4*. https://doi.org/10.25517/jhnr.v4i0

Brughmans, T., & Peeples, M. (2023). *Network science in archaeology*. Cambridge University Press. https://doi:10.1017/9781009170659

Collar, A. (2013). *Religious networks in the Roman empire: The spread of new ideas*. Cambridge University Press. https://doi.org/10.1017/CBO9781107338364

Freeman, L. (2004). *The development of social network analysis: A study in the sociology of science*. Empirical Press.

Freeman, L. (2011). The development of social network analysis: With an emphasis on recent events. In J. Scott & P. J. Carrington (Eds.), *The Sage handbook of social network analysis* (pp. 26–39). Sage.

Goddeeris, A. (2022). Women and their weight. Incorporating weighted edges in a network analysis of the central redistributive household of Nippur (eighteenth century BCE). In K. De Graef, A. Garcia-Ventura, A. Goddeeris, & B. A. Nakhai (Eds.), *The mummy under the bed. Essays on gender and methodology in the ancient near East* (pp. 369–406). Zaphon.

Graham, S. (2006). *EX FIGLINIS: The network dynamics of the Tiber Valley brick industry in the hinterland of Rome*. British Archaeological Reports. https://doi.org/10.30861/9781841717388

Introduction 7

Jones, C. (2021). *Power and elite competition in the Neo-Assyrian empire, 745-612 BC* [Unpublished doctoral dissertation]. Columbia University.

King, R., & Pirngruber, R. (2022). Slavery in Achaemenid-Period Babylonia: The social world of Rībat, son of Bēl-Erība. *Journal of Ancient Near Eastern History*, 9(1), 113–145. https://doi.org/10.1515/janeh-2020-0025

Kulikov, A., Anderson, A., & Veldhuis, N. (2021). Sumerian networks: Classifying text groups in the Drehem archives. *IDEAH*. https://doi.org/10.21428/f1f23564.6da394df

Padgett, J. F., & Ansell, C. K. (1993). Robust action and the rise of the medici, 1400–1434. *American Journal of Sociology*, 98(6), 1259–1319. https://doi.org/10.1086/230190

Pagé-Perron, É. (2018). Network analysis for reproducible research on large administrative cuneiform corpora. In V. B. Juloux, A. R. Gansell, & A. di Ludovico (Eds.), *CyberResearch on the ancient near east and neighboring regions. Case studies on archaeological data, objects, texts, and digital archiving* (pp. 194–223). Brill. https://doi.org/10.1163/9789004375086_008

Ruffini, G. R. (2008). *Social networks in Byzantine Egypt*. Cambridge University Press. https://doi.org/10.1017/CBO9780511552014

Scott, J. (2012). *What is social network analysis?*. Bloomsbury Academic. https://doi.org/10.5040/9781849668187

Smith, R. M. (1979). Kin and neighbors in a thirteenth-century Suffolk Community. *Journal of Family History*, 4(3), 219–256. https://doi.org/10.1177/036319907900400301

Still, B. (2019). *The social world of the Babylonian Priest*. Brill. https://doi.org/10.1163/9789004399969

Stefanović, D. (2020). Review of *The ties that bind. Ancient politics and network research*. BMCR 2020.11.34. https://bmcr.brynmawr.edu/2020/2020.11.34/

Svärd, S., Alstola, T., Jauhiainen, H., Sahala, A., & Lindén, K. (2020). Fear in Akkadian texts: New digital perspectives on lexical semantics. In S.-W. Hsu & J. Llop-Raduà (Eds.), *The expression of emotions in ancient Egypt and Mesopotamia* (pp. 470–502). Brill. https://doi.org/10.1163/9789004430761_019

Svärd, S., Jauhiainen, H., Sahala, A., & Lindén, K. (2018). Semantic domains in Akkadian texts. In V. B. Juloux, A. R. Gansell, & A. di Ludovico (Eds.), *CyberResearch on the ancient near east and neighboring regions. Case studies on archaeological data, objects, texts, and digital archiving* (pp. 224–256). Brill. https://doi.org/10.1163/9789004375086_009

Waerzeggers, C. (2014). Social network analysis of cuneiform archives – A new approach. In H. D. Baker & M. Jursa (Eds.), *Documentary sources in ancient near eastern and Greco-Roman economic history: Methodology and practice* (pp. 116–130). Oxbow Books. https://doi.org/10.2307/j.ctvh1dn9m.14

Wagner, A., Levavi, Y., Kedar, S., Abraham, K., Cohen, Y., & Zadok, R. (2013). Quantitative Social Network Analysis (SNA) and the study of cuneiform archives: A test-case based on the Murašû archive. *Akkadica*, 134, 117–134.

Weingart, S. (2011). Demystifying networks, parts I & II. *Journal of Digital Humanities*. http://journalofdigitalhumanities.org/1-1/demystifying-networks-by-scott-weingart/

2 Social Network Analysis – a brief overview

Social Network Analysis (SNA) is a method developed in the mid-XX century in mathematics, anthropology, and sociology, and is used to describe, analyse, and measure human relations.[1] However, its roots can be traced back to the end of the XIX century and research on social structures and social links by Émile Durkheim and Ferdinand Tönnies.[2] The works of Jacob Moreno, William Lloyd Warner, and Elton Mayo, as well as of Alfred Radcliffe-Brown, exemplifying the three leading traditions in network studies, marked the early decades of the XX century.[3]

Jacob Moreno is particularly important among these scholars. Along with Helen Hall Jennings he developed sociometry, a technique obtained by applying quantitative methods that inquire into the development and organisation of individual groups and the position of single actors within them.[4] His major achievement was the invention of a *sociogram* as a way to represent the formal properties of social configurations. The sociogram has become one of the most powerful innovations in network analysis, because it enables the visualisation of social networks.

With Alfred Radcliffe-Brown's stress on the concept of 'social structure,' and the idea that social actions were organised, studies of social networks came to the fore.[5] In the 1960s and the 1970s, a significant number of researchers worked on the implementation of various theories and concepts for the study of social interactions and connections, leading to Social Network Analysis. For example, Stanley Milgram developed the concept of 'six degrees of separation,' and Mark Granovetter elaborated on the theory of the 'strength of weak ties' within the network.[6] Since then, the body of research on Social Network Analysis has grown significantly, and academic journals, textbooks, vocabulary, and an increasing sophistication in its technical tools have been developed.[7]

The data, or better to say datasets, analysed through the network approach can be perceived in different ways – to identify 'missing links,' to model and detect communities and clusters, to visualise results in more comprehensive ways, and to interpret them anew. But where should it begin?

DOI: 10.4324/9781003457015-2

The starting point of any Social Network Analysis approach is to define two core elements of any given network: *nodes* and *edges*. A *node* is an 'actor' in a given network. They can represent people, places, artefacts, deities, emotions, types of pottery, commodities, workshops, etc. – whatever can be linked together. *Edges*, which may be defined by any content (e.g., kinship, exchange, patronage, friendship, strength, emotional value, distribution pattern, etc.) are links or ties between *nodes*. Consequently, the network represents a set of *nodes* and *ties* that unite them; the SNA is used to study *nodes* linked together through social or other models of interaction in order to quantify and measure interconnectivity. If the tie transmits information from one node to another, that is, if it is directed, it is called an 'edge.' By using network theory to understand social relationships, Social Network Analysis exemplifies various types of interactions through networks (*ego-networks* and *complex networks*) and analyses them to provide an overview of the networks in which selected entities, that is, nodes, manifest themselves.[8]

Depending on the analysed datasets, *ego-networks* (having one individual as a main node) and *complex networks* (focusing on a group of multiple actors) are the most common. It depends on the researcher and the available corpus of datasets, and how far away in network reconstruction one can go. When possible, the *snowball* method (implemented by adding or enlarging initial sets of nodes and edges and establishing accompanying mini ego-networks of as many individuals as possible) may be very useful.[9]

The accumulation of individual data, information, material resources, or power can be traced from node to node through edges, representing the specific types of relationships between them. Edges can be directed and weighted, providing further data on the analysed network. Thus, by collecting information and analysing the links between actors, networks and their inner structures can be identified. However, we should keep in mind that our fragmentally preserved sources may significantly restrict the amount of data available to help create and visualise any given network.

The first step in preparing datasets for the network approach is to transfer data from the database to the files or lists that are required to build a network model. Two lists with relevant information about the studied entities and the relational data that connect them are required: a *node list* and an *edge list*.[10] Their contents will vary depending on the type of nodes to be studied, the nature of the relations that should represent their interconnectivity, and the quantity and quality of information provided by sources. Nodes and edges can also be assigned more precisely with labels referred to as *node* and *edge attributes*. *Node attributes* can be both qualitative (e.g. gender, profession, rank or status marker, residence, etc.) and quantitative (e.g. age). Similarly, qualitative and quantitative *edge attributes* can provide additional information regarding the relations connecting the clusters of nodes. As such, the node and edge lists that are required for network analysis usually contain all the necessary (and available) sets of data for identifying nodes and the relational data that qualify the segments that will be incorporated in a network model and, through quantification, characterise the modelled network.

The next step in the process of network creation is to transfer a created node and edge list into a visual/graphical platform (UCINET, Gephi, NodeXL Pro, NetDraw, PAJEC, etc.) and to create graphs (a mathematical tool that draws relevant connections in quantifiable terms between our present state of affairs and the ancient primary sources) presenting the data visually, or to create a *sociogram*. Once the initial network is visualised, the software can be used to highlight and feature its chosen characteristics (through various algorithms) and present statistical values.[11]

The structural characteristics of the network, such as *density* and *centralization*, along with the properties of individual nodes, such as *degree* and *rank*, can be quantified using statistical and modelling applications.[12] The sociogram would enable us to consider a given network both from the *micro* (from the perspective of each individual entity) and *macro* perspectives (exemplifying a broader context of relationships between the chosen entities). According to S. Wasserman and K. Faust, the macro level would also enable:

> a precise way to define important social concepts, a theoretical alternative to the assumption of independent social actors, and a framework for testing theories about structured social relationships. The methods of network analysis provide explicit formal statements and measures of social structural properties that might otherwise be defined only in metaphorical terms. Such phrases as webs of relationships, closely knit networks of relations, social role, social position, group, clique, popularity, isolation, prestige, prominence, and so on are given mathematical definitions by social network analysis.[13]

Another important aspect regarding the structure of an envisaged network needs to be explained. Two types of networks, relating to the nature of the nodes, can be created.[14] A one-mode, or monopartite network (where *nodes* are, for example, persons attested on objects, and *edges* are connections among them), and two-mode, or bipartite network (where nodes are, for example, institutions and individuals attached to them, or objects and distribution sites, etc.). By using software, a bipartite network can be collapsed into a monopartite network. Making a one-mode projection of a bipartite graph may be useful because measurements that may help to quantify and objectify social relations – for example, density and centrality indices – can be calculated within one-mode graphs only.

Since various types of networks can be modelled and studied, a range of network analytical software solutions have also been developed. For example, some are particularly useful for analysing trade networks requiring spatial analysis, whereas others are better suited for the exploration of dynamic networks, offering meaningful ways to display diachronic development in networks.[15]

However, certain algorithms are generally used. *Density* measures the number of links (or edges) actually realised in a given network. A dense network is an indication of a rather cohesive world where everybody knows everybody. In addition to density, *multiplexity* and *symmetry* are properties that provide important data. Multiplexity refers to the number of relationships that activate the same edge.[16] The feature of symmetry reflects the direction of edges between nodes: if a link flows from one node to another, we have an asymmetrical tie; if it goes in both directions the relationship is symmetrical.

The number of links connected to a node is known as its *degree*, with the number of links feeding into a node known as the *in degree*, and the number of links leaving it known as the *out degree*. Specifically, the degree of a node is a numerical measure of its contacts.[17] Individuals (when a node is a person) with a high degree have a more central position in the network, and consequently they influence centralisation measures at the network level.[18] The more degree increases between two entities, the more frequently their names appear in the same 'source.' Therefore, the higher the node degree rank, the more connected the node is. For example, if the 'person X' has the highest number of links, her/his place will be the most prominent within the network.

Along with node rank, network *centrality* is one of the most widely studied and basic tools for analysing social networks.[19] Centrality should answer the question of who is the most central node in the network – the more central the position one node has, the more influence in the given network will be indicated. The degree centrality for a given node can be calculated using the following formula:

$$DC(k) = \sum_{l=1}^{n} x_{kl} = \sum_{k=1}^{n} x_{lk}$$

In this formula $DC(k)$ represents the degree centrality score for actor k, while n represents the number of nodes in the network; x is the amount of all ties. As summarized by Prell, degree centrality is calculated by binary (to all connections is given a weight of 1, and to non-connections a weight of 0) and symmetrical (the all connections are assumed to be bi-directional) data – therefore it does not consider the direction of edges or the frequency of the envisaged 'communication.'[20]

Linton Freeman introduced the concept of the three types of centralities.[21] *Degree centrality* is the simplest of the three, and the most basic mode of measuring the centrality of an individual node according to the number of connections it has to others. The higher the degree centrality score, the more links and connections a node has. Degree centrality can also produce a measure of remoteness, or inverse proximity, which can be understood as inverse

12 Social Network Analysis – a brief overview

centrality – when the nodes that are at the periphery of a network (i.e., the most distant from the focal ego) are the least central and vice versa.

The second form of centrality, *betweenness*, offers a more precise way to measure the *centrality* of a node. The betweenness of a certain actor in a network reflects the path of a minimal length that connects him/her and other nodes. The higher the *betweenness centrality* score, the more important is the actor as a bridging node within a network. This leads to another important feature of the network structure – the concept of 'bridges.'

A 'bridge' in a network can be either a 'weak' or 'strong' tie; in this case 'strength' and 'weakness' refer to the number of the connections. Why are *bridges* important?[22] Location in networks is crucial to understanding power and influence, and to detect meaningful groups of individuals from the sources; those that serve as bridges (may) hold some form of a monopoly on information or resource transmission, and thus their position increases their social capital within the network – in reality, within the analysed social, political, collegial, clientelistic, or kin groups.[23]

The formula for calculating the betweenness centrality, which is relevant for directed links although not considering their weight, for envisaged nodes x, i, and j, is as follows:

$$BC(x) = \sum \frac{\partial_{ixj}}{\partial_{ij}}, i \neq j \neq x$$

Closeness is the third of Freeman's concepts of centrality. Closeness is defined as the time or distance that it takes for information to 'travel' from one node to

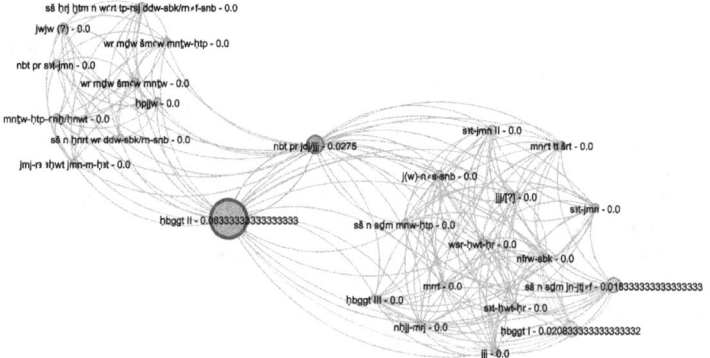

Figure 2.1 Betweenness centrality of nodes in a directed graph

another, that is, to connect them or to flow to any part of the given network.[24] In fact, it shows how quickly an actor can reach someone else in the network. The higher the closeness centrality score, the closer the actor is to all the other nodes in the network. At the same time, greater proximity means more power and theoretically may imply more capability or influence. The concepts of closeness and betweenness are very similar, and may be confusing. However, *closeness* is related to distance, whereas *betweenness* is about bridging points.

If the actors in a network are humans, the nodes representing them 'have' *centrality* and *betweenness*. They manifest a sort of influence or power, or, as exemplified by Pierre Bourdieu, 'social capital.'[25] On the other hand, if the modelled network manifests 'structural holes' (a gap between nodes, limited number of links between particular nodes, high concertation of nodes within one ego-network, etc.), it may be an indication of a specific network structure. Consequently, the modelled network may reflect a specific social structure from a given period. When combined with traditional methodological approaches, the analysed dataset may be better understood through the revealed patterns of relatedness.

Centralisation is the degree to which a network is concentrated on a single node or group of nodes.[26] This measure enables one to locate the centre of the network, as opposed to its supposed periphery, and to identify its most prominent node, nodes, or cliques. Those are not necessarily the nodes with the most connections, as will be seen from the graphs analysed in Chapter 5, but also individuals connected to the 'important persons' and those who establish a link between isolated units which occupy important positions.

Weak ties are another important element in a network. They can be defined as loose connections or bridges between different and sometimes even distant clusters of nodes. Mark Granovetter pointed out that weak ties could be extremely powerful at facilitating diffusion of resources or information across a network, allowing some nodes to directly access otherwise separate clusters or inversely central nodes.[27]

Modularity, which makes it possible to identify clusters of nodes within a network, is another important algorithm enabled by software.[28] To mark clusters within the network means to recognise a group of a minimum of three nodes, each of which needs to be linked to all the others. Furthermore, at least one of these must be connected to a node in another cluster. As outlined by Granovetter, "the strength of a tie linking clusters, or any nodes, is a combination of the amount of time, the emotional intensity, the intimacy and the reciprocal services which characterize the tie."[29] A clustering coefficient is a measure of the degree to which nodes in a graph tend to cluster. This is an important indication of the level of cohesiveness within the clique – as more neighbouring nodes are connected as the clustering coefficient increases.

Some network structures, such as the 'small-world' model, are particularly useful as models to exemplify how society may function, and have become widespread in archaeological and historical interpretations. A small-world network is a mathematical graph in which most nodes are not neighbours of one another, but the neighbours of any given node are likely to be neighbours of each other. Henceforth, most neighbouring nodes can be reached from every other node using a small number of connections or steps. Since the small-world networks tend to contain cliques, a number of separate network clusters – each comprising nodes connected to each other by 'strong ties' – are often linked by a few 'weak ties.'[30] As already exemplified, 'weak ties' act as bridging links between distant and separate groups, enabling any type of 'contact' between clusters.

As mentioned above, Social Network Analysis may be a powerful tool for analysing, examining, and testing patterns of relatedness and complex social, political, economic, and various other processes involving individual and/ or multiple actors and/or actants. *Visualisation* is one of its most important aspects. In addition to the statistical results of the measured elements, visualisation (or, it is easier to say, the graphs themselves) can instantly provide researchers with an overview of organizational structures and flow(s), as well as of patterns of relatedness between actors (or actants) on multiple levels.[31] Structural patterns such as clusters, cliques, bridges, centres, and peripheries can be immediately discerned in the graph.[32] Network visualisations offer researchers the possibility of recognising potentially new findings that may have been overlooked within the original source material(s). Features that are not readily apparent either from reading sources or from looking at charts may become evident at a first glance from the graph. Furthermore, instead of looking at objects, individuals, sites, etc., in isolation, through the lens of the network perspective we can consider their relatedness.

Many methods and algorithms derived from network analysis can be effectively applied to archaeological and historical datasets, which has led to the development of historical network research. As available software programs have not been created for past networks, archaeologists and historians (including Egyptologists) have adapted existing tools and methods that have already proven to be useful for studying other social phenomena for their own research. Given that the datasets available for research of the ancient world are by rule more or less incomplete, any created network model will be characterised or eroded by the incompleteness of the information available from the sources.[33] At first sight, it may appear as a serious obstacle, but in reality, it is very often possible to learn from an incomplete model, or from a network with 'structural holes,' just as much as from a complete network. Cristina Rosillo-López even argues that the most important new historical network research discoveries are to be made through studying negative networks.[34]

It is also important to point out that networks created from datasets originating from sources (both written and material) from the ancient world (including Egyptology) are often structured as bipartite networks linking human and non-human (institutions, tombs, sites, workshops, type of objects, etc.) nodes. In such cases, the Social Network Analysis approach is insufficient.

Actor-Network Theory (ANT), which incorporates a symmetry of agency between human and non-human participants, based on the premise that inanimate objects actively participate in shaping society, is more comprehensible.[35] Within an ANT framework, humans and non-humans share the same network through which relational action emerges.[36] Where SNA stresses networked individualism, ANT eliminates the ideas of privilege, causal relationships, and technological determinism. Actor-Network Theory makes it possible to acknowledge that there are human and non-human actors in a network, which is of crucial significance for historical and archaeological datasets. If the focus of Social Network Analysis is on the issue of 'how actors are related to each other,' Actor-Network Theory is about the way entities (human and non-human) shape each other, and how non-human elements have agency to the point where they become as important as humans.[37] For Bruno Latour, Social Network Analysis is a way to provide "information on the relations of humans in a social and natural world," whereas Actor-Network Theory seeks to account "for the very essence of societies and nature."[38] Michael Zell further stresses that "the central distinguishing feature of Actor-Network-Theory is the role that objects play in its redefinition of the social realm. The method embraces objects as participants or actors in creating, sustaining, and extending social ties, and thus is an effort to overhaul notions of society as being constituted exclusively of human interactions."[39]

Therefore, Actor-Network Theory removes any vestige of privilege, which annihilates limits on knowledge, and eliminates the 'tyranny of distance.'[40] However, ANT has also been heavily criticised for many reasons.[41] With all their positive and negative connotations, as with any other theoretical and methodological concepts, both Social Network Analysis and Actor-Network Theory provoke many *pro* and *contra* arguments, and a cautious approach is most advisable.

Nicholas Christakis and James Fowler rightly stress that network approaches provide a distinct way of seeing the world, because they are about individuals and groups and how individuals become groups.[42] Social Network Analysts observe society through its structure, and try to uncover and detect its various patterns. Since individuals are not part of just one network but of many others, they are constantly shifting, expanding, overlapping, and finally converging with society itself. For understanding any ancient society, both on the micro and macro level, that may be of essential value.

Despite the rightful assertion of Anna Collar that there must be awareness "that a representation of a network drawn from selected data does not necessarily represent a past network,"[43] network analysis is also valid with incomplete datasets. As M. Alexander and J. Danowski pointed out, the purpose of Social Network Analysis is not to claim certainty (i.e., always the case, never the case), but rather to demonstrate that something is considerably common or rare.[44] For a historian of the ancient world, including Egyptologists, modelled networks (and visualised graphs) should be considered as a snapshot of the research rather than the final result – indeed, a very inspiring and challenging snapshot.

Notes

1. For an introduction to Social Network Analysis (SNA) see Barabási (2003); Freeman (2004); Prell (2012); Newman (2018); Brughmans and Peeples (2023).
2. Durkheim (1893); Tönnies (1887).
3. Moreno (1951); Mayo and Warner (1945); Radcliffe-Brown (1952).
4. Moreno (1953). See also Freeman (2004), 37.
5. Radcliffe-Brown (1952), 61–67.
6. Granovetter (1973) and (1983); Milgram (1977).
7. The most important terms specific to SNA jargon are mainly based on the glossary of Brughmans and Peeples (2023), 294–309.
8. Newman (2018), 398–415; Prell (2012), 96–196; Brughmans and Peeples (2023), 1–101.
9. Wasserman and Faust (1994), 84–101.
10. For the very comprehensive overview see Brughmans and Peeples (2023), 64–99. Depending on the size and characteristics of a network, the node and edge lists can also be built directly into the chosen software (for example, in NodeXL Pro). If created separately or exported from the database, the lists are saved eider as .csv-files or .exel files (which works well with Gephi) and imported into the software for conversion into network models.
11. A wide array of Social Network Analysis software is now available, most of which is free. For a comparison of the best and most popular software, see Scott (2012), 103–110; Jokar et al. (2016); Brughmans and Peeples (2023), 291–293.
12. It should be stressed that network analysis uses mathematical algorithms and calculations to measure and analyse network structures. For any researcher, if they are to work without the help of an IT specialist, it is important to have a basic understanding of not only what the given measurements and algorithms do, but also how they arrive at the results.
13. Wasserman and Faust (1994), 17.
14. For an overview see Brughmans and Peeples (2023).
15. See Brughmans and Peeples (2023).
16. For example, a relationship between two individuals interacting socially, economically, and professionally is multiplex.
17. Rutherford (2007), 26; Brughmans and Peeples (2023), 107–111.
18. Borgatti (2005).
19. Brughmans and Peeples (2023), 132–139.
20. Prell (2012), 97–99.
21. Freeman (1979), 217–219.
22. Brughmans and Peeples (2023), 123–125.
23. Social capital is a network of relationships among people who live and work in a particular society, enabling that society to function effectively.
24. Freeman (1979), 225; Brughmans and Peeples (2023), 138–139.
25. Bourdieu & Wacquant (1992).
26. Brughmans and Peeples (2023), 133, 144.
27. Granovetter (1973), 1369.
28. Newman and Girvan (2004); Brughmans and Peeples (2023), 132; Peeples et al. (2016).
29. Granovetter (1973), 1361.
30. Watts and Strogatz (1998); Brughmans and Peeples (2023), 19, 122.
31. Brughmans and Peeples (2023), 193–237.

32 Newman et al. (2006), 213.
33 Cline (2012), 66. Many excellent introductions to the processes of doing network analysis with archaeological or historical datasets, and practical tutorials, can be accessed at https://archaeologicalnetworks.wordpress.com/resources/ (accessed August 16, 2023). See also Knappett (2011), 2020; Brughmans et al. (2016); Brughmans and Peeples (2023), 263–281; Collar (2020), and (2022).
34 Rosillo-López (2020).
35 Actor-Network Theory (ANT), advocated most notably by Bruno Latour, John Law, and Michel Callon, among many others, is a radical theory developed in sociology as a non-anthropocentric 'semiotics of materiality,' which incorporates the active role of non-human aspects of society – objects, institutions, ideas, places, etc. – into relational networks of human and non-human participants.
36 See Collar (2020), 56.
37 Vicsek et al. (2016).
38 Latour (1996), 369.
39 Zell (2011), 2–3.
40 Latour (1996), 377.
41 See Malafouris (2013), 123–149; Knappett (2005), 74–79; Knappett (2018) and (2020); Collar (2020), 50; Van Oyen (2015). For ANT and Egyptology see Matić (2016) and Fitzenreiter (2023).
42 Christakis and Fowler (2010), 32.
43 Collar (2020), 50.
44 Alexander and Danowski (1990).

References

Alexander, M., & Danowski, J. (1990). Analysis of an ancient network: Personal communication and the study of social structure in a past society. *Social Networks*, *12*(4), 313–335. https://doi.org/10.1016/0378-8733(90)90013-Y
Barabási, A.-L. (2003). *Linked: The new science of networks*. Perseus Publishing.
Borgatti, S. P. (2005). Centrality and network flow. *Social Networks*, *27*(1), 55–71. https://doi.org/10.1016/j.socnet.2004.11.008
Bourdieu, P., & Wacquant, L. J. D. (1992). *An invitation to reflexive sociology*. The University of Chicago Press.
Brughmans, T., & Peeples, M. (2023). *Network science in archaeology*. Cambridge University Press. https://doi:10.1017/9781009170659
Brughmans, T., Collar, A., & Coward, F. (Eds.). (2016). *The connected past: Challenges to network studies in archaeology and history*. Oxford University Press. https://doi.org/10.1093/oso/9780198748519.001.0001
Christakis, N., & Fowler, J. (2010). *Connected: The amazing power of social networks and how they shape our lives*. Harper Press.
Cline, D. (2012). Six degrees of Alexander: Social network analysis as a tool for ancient history. *Ancient History Bulletin*, *26*(1), 59–70.
Collar, A. (2020). Networks, connectivity, and material culture. In C. Cooper (Ed.), *New approaches to ancient material culture in the Greek & Roman world. 21st-century methods and classical antiquity* (pp. 47–62). Brill. https://doi.org/10.1163/9789004440753_003
Collar, A. (2022). Strong ties, social networks, and the diffusion of new ideas. Who do you trust?. In A. Collar (Ed.), *Networks and the spread of ideas in the past strong*

ties, innovation and knowledge exchange (pp. 1–27). Routledge. https://doi.org/10.4324/9780429429217

Durkheim, E. (1893). *De la division du travail social*. F. Alcan.

Fitzenreiter, M. (2023). *Technology and culture in Pharaonic Egypt: Actor network theory and the archaeology of things and people*. Cambridge University Press. https://doi:10.1017/9781009070300

Freeman, L. (1979). Centrality in social networks: Conceptual clarification. *Social Networks, 1*(3), 215–239. https://doi.org/10.1016/0378-8733(78)90021-7

Freeman, L. (2004). *The development of social network analysis: A study in the sociology of science*. Empirical Press.

Granovetter, M. (1973). The strength of weak ties. *American Journal of Sociology, 78*(6), 1360–1380. http://www.jstor.org/stable/2776392

Granovetter, M. (1983). The strength of weak ties: A network theory revisited. In R. Collins (Ed.), *Sociological theory* (pp. 201–233). Collins Press.

Jokar, N., Honarvar, A. R., Esfandiari, K., & Shima Aghamirzadeh, S. (2016). The review of social networks analysis tools. *Bulletin de la Societe Royale des Sciences de Liege, 85*, 329–339. https://doi.org/10.25518/0037-9565.5380

Knappett, C. (2005). *Thinking through material culture: An interdisciplinary perspective. Archaeology, culture, and society*. University of Pennsylvania Press. http://www.jstor.org/stable/j.ctt3fhh6q

Knappett, C. (2011). *An archaeology of interaction: Network perspectives on material culture and society*. Oxford University Press. https://doi.org/10.1093/acprof:osobl/9780199215454.001.0001

Knappett, C. (2018). From network connectivity to human mobility: Models for minoanization. *Journal of Archaeological Method and Theory, 25*(4), 974–995. https://doi.org/10.1007/s10816-018-9396-9

Knappett, C. (2020). Relational concepts and challenges to network analysis in social archaeology. In L. Donnellan (Ed.), *Archaeological networks and social interaction* (pp. 20–37). Routledge. https://doi.org/10.4324/9781351003063

Latour, B. (1996). On actor-network theory: A few clarifications. *Soziale Welt, 47*(4), 369–381. http://www.jstor.org/stable/40878163

Malafouris, L. (2013). *How things shape the mind: A theory of material engagement*. The MIT Press. https://doi.org/10.7551/mitpress/9476.001.0001.

Matić, U. (2016). (De)queering Hatshepsut: Binary bind in archaeology of Egypt and kingship beyond the corporeal. *Journal of Archaeological Method & Theory, 23*(3), 810–831. https://doi.org/10.1007/s10816-016-9288-9

Mayo, E., & Warner, W. L. (1945). *The social problems of an industrial civilization*. Harvard University Press.

Milgram, S. (1977). *The individual in a social world: Essays and experiments*. Addison-Wesley.

Moreno, J. L. (1951). *Sociometry, experimental method and the science of society: An approach to a new political orientation*. Beacon House.

Moreno, J. L. (1953). *Who shall survive?: Foundations of sociometry, group psychotherapy and sociodrama*. Beacon House.

Newman, M. E. J. (2018). *Networks*. Oxford University Press. https://doi.org/10.1093/oso/9780198805090.001.0001

Newman, M. E. J., & Girvan, M. (2004). Finding and evaluating community structure in networks. *Physical Review E: Statistical, Nonlinear, and Soft Matter Physics, 69*(2), 1–15. https://doi.org/10.1103/PhysRevE.69.026113

Newman, M. E. J., Barabási, A.-L., & Watts, D. J. (2006). *The structure and dynamics of networks*. Princeton University Press. http://www.jstor.org/stable/j.ctt7ssgv

Peeples, M. A., Mills, B. J., Haas, W. R. J., Clark, J. J., & Roberts, J. M. J. (2016). Analytical challenges for the application of social network analysis in archaeology. In T. Brughmans, A. Collar, & F. Coward (Eds.), *The connected past: Challenges to network studies in archaeology and history* (pp. 59–84). Oxford University Press. https://doi.org/10.1093/9780198748519.003.0010

Prell, C. (2012). *Social network analysis: History, theory and methodology*. Sage Publications.

Radcliffe-Brown, A. R. (1952). *Structure and function in primitive society: Essays and addresses*. Cohen & West.

Rosillo-López, C. (2020). Informal political communication and network theory in the late Roman republic. *Journal of Historical Network Research, 4*, 90–113. https://doi.org/10.25517/jhnr.v4i0.75

Rutherford, J. (2007). Network theory and theoric networks. *Mediterranean Historical Review, 22*(1), 23–37. https://doi.org/10.1080/09518960701538523

Scott, J. (2012). *What is social network analysis?*. Bloomsbury Academic. https://doi.org/10.5040/9781849668187

Tonnies, F. (1887). *Gemeinschaft und Gesellschaft: Abhandlung des Communismus und des Socialismus als empirischer Culturformen*. Fues.

Van Oyen, A. (2015). Actor-network theory's take on archaeological types: Becoming, material agency, and historical explanation. *Cambridge Archaeological Journal, 25*(1), 63–78. https://doi.org/10.1017/S0959774314000705

Vicsek, L., Király, G., & Kónya, H. (2016). Networks in the social sciences. *Corvinus Journal of Sociology and Social Policy, 7*(2), 77–102. https://doi.org/10.14267/cjssp.2016.02.04

Wasserman, S., & Faust, K. (1994). *Social network analysis: Methods and applications*. Cambridge University Press. https://doi.org/10.1017/CBO9780511815478

Watts, D. J., & Strogatz, S. H. (1998). Collective dynamics of "small-world" networks. *Nature, 393*(6684), 440–442. https://doi:10.1038/30918

Zell, M. (2011, Summer). Rembrandt's gifts: A case study of actor-network-theory. *Journal of Historians of Netherlandish Art, 3*(2). https://doi.org/10.5092/jhna.2011.3.2.2

3 A long-short way from Ruffini's *Social Networks in Byzantine Egypt*

Historians often choose, for many reasons, a chronological approach to the topics they have decided to explore. This chapter will not be an exception, following the periodisation of the dynastic history of Ancient Egypt.[1]

In 1996, Charles Wetherell and Barry Wellman argued in an article published in the journal *History of the Family* that network studies offered important new ways of conceptualising communities.[2] Two years later, Wetherell stressed in the *International Review of Social History* that Social Network Analysis offered 'real potential' for social historians, providing new approaches to the study of kinship and village communities.[3] However, Egyptology had to wait 20 years to implement the Social Network Analysis methodology.

In 2008, Cambridge University Press published a book titled *Social Networks in Byzantine Egypt* by Giovanni Roberto Ruffini.[4] The book, originating from the author's PhD dissertation, is a prosopographic overview of the settlements of Oxyrhynchos and Aphrodito (with a focus on social structure) from the second half of the V century through the Arab conquest of Egypt.

The two sites chosen by Ruffini are very different. Oxyrhynchos was the metropolis of a nome, and since the V century it has been the capital of the province of Arcadia. Over the course of time, Aphrodito decreased in status from the *metropolis* of the *nome* to the *village* (*kome*). The social structure of the two places also reflects a significant difference. The same is true for the quantity and quality of the preserved written sources. Those originating from Oxyrhynchos mainly consist of documents from the administrative offices of large aristocratic and ecclesiastical estates. The Byzantine papyri from Aphrodito belong mainly to a family archive from the mid-seventh century.

Ruffini combined two methodological approaches: classical prosopography and Social Network Analysis. For the survey at each of the two sites, he presented one prosopographic and one SNA chapter.

The data from Oxyrhynchos highlight links in society across a broader region and an elite kinship-group (the Apions), while the data from Aphrodito, due to the preservation of a single family's archive (that of the lawyer/poet known as Dioskoros), show very close multi-layered relationships within a single village. Based on the analysed material, Ruffini also claims that scholarly focus on Dioskoros himself distracts the prosopographer from a true picture of the Aphrodito archive and all the interconnections between individuals attested in the documents. Using the network approach, he managed to change that picture, identifying the most central figures in the archive, and measuring its quantitative nature.[5]

In the case of Oxyrhynchos, Ruffini's research was based on a register of approximately 600 place-names. For Aphrodito, he created his own database, built on work by V. A. Girgis, starting from a prosopographic index of nearly 2,000 inhabitants of a village.[6]

Ruffini created two-mode networks using UCINET software, combining individuals (or places) and documents as nodes. With the Social Network Analysis approach, he was able to highlight a few of the most central actors in the network and shed new light on important individuals who had been previously obscured by scholars mostly focused on Dioskoros and his family. Ruffini also draws attention to groups with 'high tie strengths.'

It is important to stress that Ruffini's book is at the same time the first to apply SNA methodology on datasets originating from Egypt, and taken in a broader context, the first in the realm of Egyptology.

The initial novelty of the book was most vividly exemplified by the opening sentence of the review written by Andrea Jördens: "Dies ist ein Buch, das vor noch wenigen Jahren so vermutlich nicht hätte geschrieben werden können."[7]

And the reason behind this statement is Ruffini's implementation of Social Network Analysis, which allowed him to "measure the extent of a society's centralization, to identify topographical patterns in the formation of its large estates, and to identify the most central ... figures in its social networks."[8]

The results presented in *Social Networks in Byzantine Egypt* were mostly welcomed, and Conor Whatelys marked this study as "an important and provocative addition to modern scholarship on the social history of late antiquity."[9] However, Whatelys also stated that "some will find fault with Ruffini's usage of modern network analysis."[10]

Such critiques were even more explicitly uttered by Roberta Mazza: "Did the application of social network analysis dramatically improve our knowledge of late-antique Egyptian society? After reading Ruffini's book, I have to say that I am not totally convinced."[11]

Indeed, many researchers expect Social Network Analysis (especially those not very familiar with the method or those sceptical towards digital humanities) to provide solutions for all scholarly misconceptions, misunderstandings, and pitfalls. Do we expect the same result from any other methodological approach?

While staying in the world of late antique Egypt, Renate Dekker's book *Episcopal Networks and Authority in Late Antique Egypt: Bishops of the Theban Region at Work* is the next to be mentioned.[12] The aim of Dekker's work, based on several datasets incorporating sources from the late VI and VII centuries, was to analyse the social networks of two bishops, i.e., Abraham of Hermonthis and Pesynthius of Coptos, and the scope and nature of their authority. Although her book was published ten years after *Social Networks in Byzantine Egypt*, Ruffini himself, in his review of *Episcopal Networks*, wrote that: "Social network analysis is the newest methodology of the three to work its way into the study of the ancient world, and still needs an introduction for most readers."[13]

The methodological 'novelty' of Dekker's work also attracted the attention of Ariel López. In his review on *Episcopal Networks* López rightly spotted that the author has used two methodologies: Social Network Analysis and the typology of the duties of the late antique bishop, established by Claudia Rapp.[14] For Lopez, the second approach is useful, whereas the first one is not:

> Too much of this book is occupied with long, jargon-filled descriptions of network properties and software analysis. In the end, they lead nowhere. So much work with so little payoff. As so often, network analysis ends up becoming an end in itself, a scholarly conceit. It neither raises new, interesting questions nor does it answer old ones. One only needs to look at the graphs at the end of the book to see this. What are they supposed to show?[15]

Indeed, what are Social Network Analysis and graphs supposed to say or to show? A hint at the answer to that question, within the field of Egyptology, came in fact several years before the review by López, in a paper written by the late Diane H. Cline and Eric H. Cline focusing on the Amarna letters, the corpus of cuneiform documents originating from the New Kingdom (c. 1550–1069 BC).

However, before an overview is given of the main publications and projects dealing with the New Kingdom datasets, recent contributions from Lena Tambs, focusing on private archives from the Ptolemaic period, need to be mentioned. Her book *Socio-Economic Relations in Ptolemaic Pathyris* is by now the most comprehensive and profound Egyptological study that implements network theory concepts and Social Network Analysis.[16] In order to analyse the corpus of 428 Greek and Demotic documents from the late Ptolemaic Period (186–188 BC) that were found in the region of Gebelein (Pathyris), Tambs combines traditional and innovative methods and theories, including SNA. Through the analysis of documents originating from 21 archives (belonging to 16 families) from the site, the complexity of various aspects of the everyday life of the community and its socioeconomic interactions emerge in many fascinating details, especially on the accompanying graphs. The networks are discussed and explained in the context of broader archaeological and historical narratives, which clearly demonstrate the potential of the chosen methodological approach. With an overview of the network approach methodology, a presentation of its potentials, an illustration of its limitations, and an elaborate demonstration of the SNA and her used software (Gephi), Tambs' book can also be recommended as a manual for all those interested in the discipline. She rightly stressed the following:

> Social Network Analysis (SNA) has not previously been employed to this extent for the purpose of addressing questions about interpersonal connectivity, human behaviour and socio-economic life in an ancient Egyptian community. As such, the project serves as a test case for a large-scale in-depth application of SNA concepts and tools to a big-data study of attribute and relational data retrieved from ancient Egyptian and Greek documents written in the late Ptolemaic Period.[17]

Interpersonal Relationships in Early Ptolemaic Egypt: A Network Analytical Study of the Zenon Archive (263–229 BCE), Tambs' ongoing project hosted by the Department of Cultures, Centre of Excellence in Ancient Near Eastern Empires (ANEE, University of Helsinki),[18] is devoted to the study of life under king Ptolemy II Philadelphus (284–246 BC), as reflected in the Zenon Archive – the largest private archive from Ancient Egypt.

Nearly 1,845 documents from a limited period of 35 years (263–229 BC) revealed detailed information about individuals living under various conditions in Egypt and beyond. In the studies published within the project, Tambs demonstrates that formal methods of SNA can be used to map, visualise, and analyse concrete examples that show how things, people, and powers move between and within regions and mutually interact.[19]

The network approach is not restricted to historical and archaeological material and can be equally applied to linguistic and philological datasets. Nico Dogaer and Mark Depauw have explored the formulaic framework of the Demotic papyrus letters, stressing that one of the greatest advantages of the network methodology is visualisation, resulting in the fact that the entire analysed corpus can be presented in one single image.[20]

The book by Håkon Fiane Teigen, *The Manichaean Church in Kellis*, built upon prosopography and network concepts, traces and analyses the social networks of the most prominent individuals in and the social dimensions of the Manichaean community, in the Oasis and the village.[21]

The paper 'Text Messages, Tablets, and Social Networks: The "Small World" of the Amarna Letters,' by the late Diane H. Cline and Eric H. Cline, explores the cohesiveness of the social network that connected the Great Powers of the Ancient Near East (i.e. Egypt, Mitanni, Hatti, Alashiya, Babylonia) during the XIV century BC through cuneiform documents from the Amarna archive.[22] Letters provide social information from both metadata and content. However, as stated by the authors, with almost 400 documents it is hardly possible to have a clear overview of all of the social ties – who wrote to whom, traded with whom, sent gifts to whom, intermarried with whom, got in quarrels with whom, and complained to the king about whom. Indeed, this was a complex network of interactions. The authors stated that:

> Social Network Analysis (or SNA) provides away to keep track of and display these social relations, allowing us to think about how the people mentioned in the tablets, and the people who sent and received them, form a network. It is, quite specifically, a method to map relationships and transactions between people or groups, understanding them collectively through data visualization.[23]

The graphs clearly and visually exemplify the complexity of political and diplomatic relationships within the worlds of the Eastern Mediterranean and Western Asia during the Late Bronze Age. Furthermore, the presented modelled networks corroborate the known historical setting based on the traditional analysis of written and archaeological material.

The same datasets were recently used by Clément Dutrey to analyse the relationships between the great kings of the Ancient Near East and the local Canaanite rulers towards the end of the XVIII Dynasty (c. 1550–1292 BC).[24]

The work of Vincent Chollier within the short history of Social Network Analysis in Egyptology deserves a special place. Based on his research on the social strategies of people attached to provincial temples during the New Kingdom (c. 1550–1069 BC), Chollier managed to exemplify the potentials of reconstructed administrative structures for the hierarchical and familial networks of individuals attached to temples.[25] The main results of his study are encompassed in his PhD dissertation *Administrer les cultes au Nouvel Empire (1539–1077 av. J.-C.): stratégies sociales et territoriales*.[26] Vincent Chollier should be also credited as the first Egyptologist, *stricto sensu*, who wrote on the possibilities and limitations of SNA in Egyptology.[27]

Anne Herzberg has published several papers through the last few years combining prosopographic data from the Ramesside Memphite necropolis with SNA, as a part of her project *Prosopographia Memphitica*.[28] Her recently published book focuses on the New Kingdom Memphite tombs.[29] A wealth of preserved personal data is the most important source of information for the population living and working in the royal residence. To draw as representative a picture of Memphis and its inhabitants as possible, prosopographic data were firstly compiled in a comprehensive corpus.[30] While combining the traditional historical approach with digital humanities tools, Herzberg treated individuals attested in sources not as isolated units but as actors who interact with each other on a social level and form social links.[31] Another important aspect of Herzberg's approach is her observation that tombs themselves can be linked through individuals recorded in the inscriptions on their walls, offering a unique perspective and the possibility to map the Memphite necropolis anew.[32]

The Second Intermediate Period's (c. 1750–1550 BC) material culture, through the lens of network analysis, has been the focus of the research of Arianna Sacco.[33] Unfortunately, the Middle Kingdom (c. 2040–1750 BC) data have not attracted much scholarly attention. The present author is focused on the social settings and interconnections of Middle Kingdom/Second Intermediate Period individuals, combining traditional prosopography and Social Network Analysis. Initial results were published in the paper 'The Social Network(s) of the Middle Kingdom and Second Intermediate Period Treasurers: Rehuerdjersen, Siese, Ikhernefret and Senebsumai.'[34] As in the case of the Amarna archive, the reconstructed networks of high-ranking officials support the already recognised patterns of the Late Middle Kingdom society.

The Old Kingdom (c. 2680–2160 BC) data have attracted increasing attention as being suitable for the application of Social Network Analysis. Émilie Martinet extensively explored the Old Kingdom provincial administration and the stratification of the local elites based on a database containing about 1500 officials, combining the network approach and traditional prosopography. The results of Martinet's research are most comprehensively outlined in her book L'Administration provinciale sous l'Ancien Empire égyptien.[35]

Émilie Martinet also noted that SNA tools may be useful for detecting and visualising already recognised patterns and features of social transformations (such as social mobility and hierarchy) during the Old Kingdom. By using the network approach, it was possible to uncover the role of some individuals in a broader context, as well as to detect the dynamics among the social groups surrounding prominent persons (usually tomb owners).[36]

A number of important contributions from Veronika Dulíková and Radek Mařík, results of a fruitful collaboration between an Egyptologist and a cybernetician, are focused on the Old Kingdom elite society. Based on the systematic recording of a vast number of prosopographic and archaeological data in a database (Maat database), which currently contains around 6,000 officials from the Memphite region, Dulíková, Mařík, and their team developed a new approach based on the analysis of complex networks in order to detect the social processes which affected the elites residing in Memphis, the capital of Egypt during the Old Kingdom.[37] For example, they introduced an index (*nepotism index*) aimed at detecting and quantifying the presence of nepotism within the elite of Memphis.[38]

Several collective volumes published in recent years, such as the proceedings of the international *Social Networks Analyses in Ancient Egypt* workshop, held in Prague in 2018,[39] and, although not exclusively dealing with networks and SNA, the *Handbook of Digital Egyptology: Texts*[40] and *Ancient Egypt, New Technology*,[41] open new venues for network research and network approach in Egyptology. Furthermore, a recently published book by Martin Fitzenreiter explores how the material culture of dynastic Egypt was shaped through the interplay of things and people – of non-human actants and human actors – and reflected in networks of entanglement of people and objects.[42]

3.1 Trismegistos

Trismegistos (TM) is an important step in the long-short joint venture of Egyptology and Social Network Analysis.[43]

Trismegistos was launched as a digital platform to facilitate interdisciplinary research on textual sources from Ancient Egypt, in particular from the Late, Graeco-Roman, and Byzantine periods (roughly from 800 BC until 800 AD).[44] The platform was initially built on databases and prosopographies, starting with the *Heidelberger Gesamtverzeichnisder griechischer Urkunden aus Ägypten*[45] and the *Leuven Database of Ancient Books*.[46] The initial idea of the platform was:

> to foster interdisciplinarity in the study of Ancient Egyptian society by creating a central database with metadata about published papyrological texts from Greco-Roman Egypt, in a first instance written in Greek, Latin and Egyptian (including hieroglyphic, hieratic and demotic).[47]

However, over the years, the wealth of collected data (languages, scripts, and writing materials), as well as the platform links with other databases, have resulted in the development of different standards for collecting and processing metadata and separating publications and tools.

Nowadays, the 'Text database' is the core around which the rest of Trismegistos is built. By expanding to other databases, such as the Prosopographia Ptolemaica,[48] Trismegistos has been able to create, since 2008, databases collecting information regarding the contents of these texts in two basic forms: TM People (i.e., people and their names) and TM Places.[49] To date TM includes almost half a million attestations of individuals in Greek and Egyptian texts originating between 800 BC and 800 AD.

The next step came in 2012, when Trismegistos began the application of network analysis to the study of social hierarchies in Ptolemaic letters and contracts.[50]

Yanne Broux, working with TM data, has produced several important contributions, establishing the so-called "onomastic networks."[51] While Trismegistos is not a prosopography, its data are structured in such a way as to allow the extraction of source and person records for two-mode networks.[52] Departing from ideas that names can be linked through family relations and that elements such as status, ethnicity, and religion are important attributes that can help explain various aspects of the social structure, Broux has completed several important studies on the prosopographic analysis, incorporating Social Network Analysis, of Greco-Egyptian naming practices.[53]

All Trismegistos networks are presented at www.trismegistos.org/network/menu.[54] TM networks are not a database but a platform presenting the networks used in research papers, where static screenshots offer substitutes for the original graphs created in Gephi and visualise the relations between the chosen data that are otherwise not always apparent. The TM Networks menu consists of two sections: 'Main courses – networks for articles,' presenting an overview of all papers written by TM associates that use a network analytical approach, and 'Side Dishes – Networks as database add-ons,' with networks containing relational information from different TM subsections. Graphs are interactive, searchable and linked to corresponding information in online databases. The networks can be displayed on a separate web page, as is the case with, for example, *Network of Names in Trismegistos People*,[55] or embedded.[56]

Trismegistos networks rely on network theory and Social Network Analysis methodology, which involves the creation of a two-mode network with written sources and persons/names, and then the production of a one-mode affiliation network, to show the relatedness of the actors.

Carl Knappett stresses in the introduction to *Network Analysis in Archaeology* that the term 'network' is not new to the discipline, but that archaeologists discussing various types of networks typically use the term generically as 'little more than a handy metaphor for connectivity.'[57] Similarly, the editors of the first volume of *The Journal of Historical Network Research*, published in 2017, noted that 'historians have until recently continued to abide by relatively vague notions of "networks" in a metaphorical sense, as a convenient image for the sum of social interactions or as an expression of a rather diffuse notion of underlying social structures.'[58]

The same applies to Egyptology as well. Although network approaches are gaining increasing attention in history and archaeology, as can be observed from the *Historical Network Research Bibliography*,[59] formal applications of network theories and concepts are still scarcely represented in Egyptology. Consequently, examples from Ancient Egypt are only occasionally included in historical network studies, and most of the large-scale applications of Social Network Analysis to the research of ancient material have been concerned with fields other than Egyptology. Although Egyptological studies have occasionally addressed relational and network-oriented questions, they have seldom used formal network analysis.[60] Notwithstanding that the future may bring some positive changes, the discipline is presently far behind Classical Studies and Assyriology.

Notes

1 Not to list all works focusing on various aspects of the network approach but to highlight major and ground-breaking contributions and ongoing projects. For a brief overview see also Martinet (2020a), 4–6.

2 Wellman and Wetherell (1996).
3 Wetherell (1998).
4 Ruffini (2008).
5 Ruffini (2008).
6 Girgis (1938). See also Ruffini (2011) and Graham and Ruffini (2007).
7 Jördens (2011), 712.
8 Ruffini (2008), 3.
9 Whatelys (2009).
10 Whatelys (2009).
11 Mazza (2009).
12 Dekker (2018).
13 Ruffini (2019), 360.
14 López (2019).
15 López (2019).
16 Tambs (2022); see also Tambs (2020).
17 Tambs (2022), 488.
18 Available from https://researchportal.helsinki.fi/en/projects/interpersonal-relationships-in-early-ptolemaic-egypt-a-network-an with further bibliographic references by the author (accessed August 16, 2023).
19 See the list at https://researchportal.helsinki.fi/en/persons/lena-tambs (accessed August 22, 2023).
20 Dogaer and Depauw (2017).
21 Teigen (2021).
22 Cline and Cline (2015); Diane H. Cline has been also applying SNA to the datasets of ancient Greek and Hellenistic history. See, for example Cline and Hasaki (2023).
23 Cline and Cline (2015), 21.
24 Dutrey (2021).
25 I am grateful to Vincent Chollier for providing me with a copy of his unpublished PhD dissertation.
26 Chollier (2017). See also Chollier (2016) and (2020).
27 Chollier (2019).
28 See Herzberg (2019) and (2020).
29 Herzberg-Beiersdorf (2023).
30 https://www.prosopographia-memphitica.com (accessed August 16, 2023).
31 Herzberg-Beiersdorf (2023).
32 Herzberg (2020).
33 Sacco (2019).
34 Stefanović (2019) and (2020).
35 Martinet (2019a).
36 Martinet (2019b) and (2020b).
37 Dulíková and Mařík (2020); Dulíková and Mařík (2021); Bárta et al. (2022).
38 Dulíková and Mařík (2017).
39 Dulíková and Bárta (2020).
40 Gracia Zamacona and Ortiz García (2021).
41 Lucarelli et al. (2023).
42 Fitzenreiter (2023).
43 See www.trismegistos.org (accessed August 16, 2023).
44 Soon after, Trismegistos expanded into the most of the ancient Mediterranean world. TM Texts now also incorporates all Latin inscriptions as well as several indigenous languages such as Arabic, Celtiberian, and Syriac (a full list is available at www.trismegistos.org/about_languages; accessed August 16, 2023).
45 See http://aquila.zaw.uni-heidelberg.de/start (accessed August 16, 2023).

46 Now www.trismegistos.org/ldab. See www.trismegistos.org/about_history for a more detailed history (accessed August 16, 2023).
47 Broux (2017), 344; see also Graham and Ruffini (2007); Broux and Pietowski (2020).
48 Connected to more than 30 other databases storing information about or mentioned in the sources.
49 www.trismegistos.org/ref and https://www.trismegistos.org/geo/ (accessed August 16, 2023).
50 Dogaer and Depauw (2017).
51 See https://kuleuven.academia.edu/YanneBroux (accessed August 16, 2023).
52 See http://www.trismegistos.org/ref/about_prosopography.php (accessed August 16, 2023).
53 Broux and Depauw (2015); Broux (2015), (2017b) and (2020).
54 Accessed August 16, 2023.
55 https://www.trismegistos.org/network/6_2015_03_13/ (accessed August 16, 2023).
56 See, for example, www.trismegistos.org/edit/detail.php?edit_id=410#editnetworks (accessed August 16, 2023).
57 Knappett (2013), 3.
58 Rollinger et al. (2017), iii.
59 See https://historicalnetworkresearch.org/bibliography/ (accessed August 16, 2023).
60 See Joanne-Marie Robinson (2020).

References

Bárta, M., Dulíková, V., Mařík, R., & Cibuľa, M. (2020). Modelling the dynamics of ancient Egyptian state during the Old Kingdom period: Hidden Markov Models and social network analysis. *Zeitschrift für Ägyptische Sprache und Altertumskunde, 149*(1), 1–16. https://doi.org/10.1515/zaes-2020-0017

Broux, Y. (2015). Graeco-Egyptian naming practices: A network perspective. *Greek, Roman, and Byzantine Studies, 55,* 706–720.

Broux, Y. (2016). Detecting settlement communities in Graeco-Roman Egypt. *The Bulletin of the American Society of Papyrologists, 53,* 295–313. https://doi.org/10 .2143/BASP.53.0.3200514.2020

Broux, Y. (2017a). Towards a universal Facebook of the ancient world. In S. Orlandi, R. Santucci, F. Mambrini, & P. M. Liuzzo (Eds.), *Digital and traditional epigraphy in context proceedings of the EAGLE 2016 international conference* (pp. 343–352). Sapienza Università Editrice.

Broux, Y. (2017b). Egyptian names and networks in Trismegistos (800 BC – AD 800). In G. Rosati & M. C. Guidotti (Eds.), *Proceedings of the XI international congress of Egyptologists, Florence, Italy 23–30 August 2015* (pp. 64–68). Archaeopress. https://doi.org/10.2307/j.ctv177tjnf.16

Broux, Y. (2020). Things can only get better for Socrates and his crocodile: How onomastics can benefit from digital humanities. *The Classical Quarterly, 69,* 825–845. https://doi.org/10.1017/S0009838820000026

Broux, Y., & Depauw, M. (2015). Developing onomastic gazetteers and prosopographies for the ancient world through named entity recognition and graph visualization: Some examples from trismegistos people. In L. M. Aiello & D. McFarland (Eds.),

Social informatics. SocInfo 2014 international workshops, Barcelona, Spain, November 11, 2014 (pp. 304–313). Springer.

Broux, Y., & Pietowski, F. (2020). Trismegistos' TOMATILLO: A new tool to visualize related data in an online environment. In M. Barta & V. Dulikova (Eds.), *Addressing the dynamics of change in ancient Egypt: Complex network analysis* (pp. 154–170). Charles University in Prague.

Chollier, V. (2016). Analyse des réseaux d'élites en Égypte ancienne. Réflexions sur des solutions méthodologiques. In R. Letricot, M. Cuxac, M. Uzcategui, & A. Cavaletto (Eds.), *Le réseau. Usages d'une notion polysémique en sciences humaines et sociales* (pp. 57–72). Presses universitaires de Louvain.

Chollier, V. (2017). *Administrer les cultes au Nouvel Empire (1539-1077 av. J.-C.): stratégies sociales et territoriales* [Unpublished doctoral dissertation]. Université de Lyon.

Chollier, V. (2019). Social network analysis in Egyptology: Benefits, methods and limits. *Journal of Egyptian Archaeology, 105*, 83–96. https://doi.org/10.1177/0307513319889329

Chollier, V. (2020). From court society to power networks: Evolution of social structures in new kingdom's upper Egypt. In M. Barta & V. Dulikova (Eds.), *Addressing the dynamics of change in ancient Egypt: Complex network analysis* (pp. 137–153). Charles University in Prague.

Cline, D. H., & Cline, E. H. (2015). Text messages, tablets, and social networks: The "small world" of the Amarna letters. In J. Mynářová, P. Onderka, & P. Pavúk (Eds.), *There and back again – The crossroads II* (pp. 17–44). Charles University in Prague.

Cline, D. H., & Hasaki, E. (2023). Assortative mixing in the social networks of Athenian Potters and the search for communities of practice. *Journal of Historical Network Research, 8*(1), 21–55. https://doi.org/10.25517/jhnr.v8i1.200

Dekker, R. (2018). *Episcopal networks and authority in late antique Egypt: Bishops of the Theban region at work*. Peeters Publishers.

Dogaer, N., & Depauw, M. (2017). Mapping the demotic epistolary framework through network visualisation. *Zeitschrift für Ägyptische Sprache und Altertumskunde, 144*(2), 173–187. https://doi.org/10.1515/zaes-2017-0011

Dulíková, V., & Bárta, M. (Eds.). (2020). *Addressing the dynamics of change in ancient Egypt: Complex network analysis*. Charles University in Prague.

Dulíková, V., & Mařík, R. (2017). Complex network analysis in Old Kingdom society: A nepotism case. In M. Bárta, F. Coppens, & J. Krejčí (Eds.), *Abusir and Saqqara in the year 2015* (pp. 63–83). Czech Institute of Egyptology.

Dulíková, V., & Mařík, R. (2020). Cyber-Egyptology: An overview of tools: Cybernetics, artificial intelligence, complex networks. In M. Barta & V. Dulikova (Eds.), *Addressing the dynamics of change in Ancient Egypt: Complex network analysis* (pp. 29–70). Charles University in Prague.

Dulíková, V., & Mařík, R. (2021). Uncovering Old Kingdom society arrangement: Detection of powerful dignitaries using complex network analysis. In C. Gracia Zamacona & J. Ortiz-García (Eds.), *Handbook of digital Egyptology: Texts* (pp. 69–102). Universidad de Alcalá.

Dutrey, C. (2021). Distribution de l'information et stratégies relationnelles dans le corpus de correspondances amarniennes: approche par l'analyse de réseaux. *Journal of Historical Network Research, 6*(1). https://doi.org/10.25517/jhnr.v6i1.85

Fitzenreiter, M. (2023). *Technology and culture in Pharaonic Egypt*. Actor network theory and the archaeology of things and people. Cambridge University Press. https://doi.org/10.1017/9781009070300

Girgis, V. A. (1938). *Prosopografia e Aphroditopolis*. Dr. Emil Ebering.

Gracia Zamacona, C. & J. Ortiz-García (Eds.). (2020). Handbook of Digital Egyptology: Texts. Universidad de Alcalá.

Graham, S., & Ruffini, G. R. (2007). Network analysis and Greco-Roman prosopography. In K. S. B. Keats-Rohan (Ed.), *Prosopography approaches and applications. A handbook* (pp. 325–336). Oxford University Press.

Herzberg, A. (2019). Prosopographia Memphitica – Analyzing prosopographical data and personal networks from the Memphite necropolis. In N. Staring, H. Twiston Davies, & L. Weiss (Eds.), *Perspectives on lived religion: Practices – Transmission – Landscape* (pp. 39–58). Sidestone Press.

Herzberg, A. (2020). Towards a Memphite prosopography of the new Kingdom – Promises and pitfalls of historical network analysis. In M. Barta & V. Dulikova (Eds.), *Addressing the dynamics of change in ancient Egypt: Complex network analysis* (pp. 105–136). Charles University in Prague.

Herzberg-Beiersdorf, A. (2023). *Prosopographia Memphitica. Individuelle Identitäten und kollektive Biographien einer königlichen Residenzstadt des Neuen Reichs*. De Gruyter. https://doi.org/10.1515/9783110783650

Jördens, A. (2011). Review of 'social networks in Byzantine Egypt'. *Gnomon, 83*, 712–715.

Knappett, C. (2013). Introduction: Why networks? In C. Knappett (Ed.), *Network analysis in archaeology: New approaches to regional interaction* (pp. 2–15). Oxford University Press. https://doi.org/10.1093/acprof:oso/9780199697090.003.0001

López, A. (2019, May 24). Review of '*Episcopal networks and authority in late antique Egypt*.' BMCR. https://bmcr.brynmawr.edu/2019/2019.05.24/

Lucarelli, R., Roberson, J. A., & Vinson, S. (Eds.). (2023). *Ancient Egypt, new technology: The present and future of computer visualization, virtual reality and other digital humanities in Egyptology*. Brill. https://doi.org/10.1163/9789004501294

Martinet, É. (2019a). *L'Administration provinciale sous l'Ancien Empire égyptien*. Brill. https://doi.org/10.1163/9789004407190

Martinet, É. (2019b). Social differentiation and degree of integration in court society: Towards sociology of the provincial elites in the Old Kingdom. In A. Delli Castelli & P. Piacentini (Eds.), *EDAL VI: Paper presented to the OKAA 7th conference, Milano, July 7, 2017* (pp. 260–273). Pontremoli Editore.

Martinet, E. (2020a). Pratique de la social network analysis en égyptologie et apports à l'étude des réseaux de relations des élites en Égypte ancienne. *Claroscuro, 19*(2), 1–28. http://hdl.handle.net/2133/20309

Martinet, É. (2020b). Analysing the dynamics among the social groups and the mechanisms of social promotion in the provinces in the late Old Kingdom: SNA methods and new research approaches. In M. Barta & V. Dulikova (Eds.), *Addressing the dynamics of change in ancient Egypt: Complex network analysis* (pp. 71–95). Charles University in Prague.

Mazza, R. (2009). Six degrees of separation: Social sciences, human hubs and papyri in Byzantine Egypt. *Journal of Roman Archaeology, 22*, 793–799. https://doi.org/10.1017/S1047759400021504

Robinson, J.-M. (2020). *'Blood Is Thicker Than Water': Non-royal consanguineous marriage in ancient Egypt. An exploration of economic and biological outcomes.* Archaeopress. https://doi.org/10.2307/j.ctv15vwjpj

Rollinger, C., Düring, M., Stark, M., & Gramsch, R. (2017). Editors' introduction. *Journal of Historical Network Research, 1*(1), i–vii. http://jhnr.uni.lu/index.php/jhnr/article/view/19

Ruffini, G. R. (2008). *Social networks in Byzantine Egypt.* Cambridge University Press. https://doi.org/10.1017/CBO9780511552014

Ruffini, G. R. (2011). *A prosopography of Byzantine Aphrodito.* American Society of Papyrologists. https://doi.org/10.3998/mpub.9749791

Ruffini, G. R. (2019). Review of 'Episcopal networks and authority in late antique Egypt'. *The Bulletin of the American Society of Papyrologists, 56*, 360–366. http://www.jstor.org/stable/45215061

Sacco, A. (2019). Game of dots: Using network analysis to examine the regionalization in the second intermediate period. In M. Bietak & S. Prell (Eds.), *The enigma of the Hyksos: Volume I* (pp. 369–396). Harrassowitz Verlag. https://doi.org/10.13173/9783447113328

Stefanović, D. (2019). The social network(s) of the Middle Kingdom and second intermediate period treasurers: Rehuerdjersen, Siese, Ikhernefret and Senebsumai. *Journal of Egyptian History, 12*, 259–287. https://doi.org/10.1163/18741665-12340054

Stefanović, D. (2020). *From ego-network to the global network – The world of the Middle Kingdom treasurer Senebi.* https://www.youtube.com/watch?v=JVWiegO76yY

Tambs, L. (2020). Ancient archives and network models: The case of Pathyris (ca. 165–88 BC). In M. Barta & V. Dulikova (Eds.), *Addressing the dynamics of change in ancient Egypt: Complex network analysis* (pp. 171–189). Charles University in Prague.

Tambs, L. (2022). *Socio-economic relations in Ptolemaic Pathyris: A network analytical approach to a bilingual community.* Brill. https://doi.org/10.1163/9789004500266

Teigen, H. F. (2021). *The Manichaean church in Kellis.* Brill. https://doi.org/10.1163/9789004459779

Wellman, B., & Wetherell, C. (1996). Social network analysis of historical communities: Some questions from the present for the past. *History of the Family, 1*(1), 97–121. https://doi.org/10.1016/S1081-602X(96)90022-6

Wetherell, C. (1998). Historical social network analysis. *International Review of Social History, 43*(S6), 125–144. https://doi.org/10.1017/S0020859000115123

Whately, C. (2009, July 25). Review of 'social networks in Byzantine Egypt'. *BMCR.* https://bmcr.brynmawr.edu/2009/2009.07.25/

4 Social Network Analysis and Egyptology – should I stay, or should I go?

The concept of networks, and Social Network Analysis (SNA) tools, have been applied to a wide range of archaeological and historical datasets and contexts, in a variety of ways and with variable outcomes. Within the last few decades, network approaches, as outlined in the previous chapter, have been progressing slowly in Egyptology.[1] Since Egyptology is not an isolated discipline, it is worth stressing that applications of network theories and methods, including SNA, to studies of the Classical and Ancient Near Eastern worlds have already identified many common characteristics of the reconstructed past networks, as well as challenges facing historical and archaeological network researchers.

The editors and authors of the volume *The Connected Past: Challenges to Network Studies in Archaeology and History* highlighted two particularly important research aspects: questions of identity and social performance, and the fragmented state of the evidence.[2] The first issue is directly related to the second one: the accuracy of reconstructed networks is directly related to the quantity and quality of available datasets – that is, to the percentage of preserved sources.

Vincent Chollier published in 2019 an article entitled 'Social Network Analysis in Egyptology: Benefits, Methods and Limits'[3] presenting the basic SNA methodology and stressing some of its benefits and obstacles when applied to ancient Egyptian material. Important contributions by Martinet, V. Dulikova, Anne Hertzberg, and especially Tambs, introduced in Chapter 3, also provide the reader with an extensive overview of the advantages and pitfalls of SNA through the material they have been working with.

The fragmentary character of preserved sources is one of the main obstacles to the creation of datasets and the implementation of network theory. SNA, like other methodologies developed by social sciences, is intended for analysing *actual* social structures, and we are interested in *past* social structures. How should this gap be bridged?

The scarcity of ancient Egyptian sources, the fact that most of them belong to a very specific sphere of human activities both at the individual and institutional levels (tombs, votive objects, temple inscriptions, etc.), with very few exceptions providing a glimpse into the activities of non-elite populations (such as sources originating from Lahun, Amarna, or Deir el Medina), certainly outlines a fragmentary reconstructed version of the real world.[4] Consequently, any network created from such an incomplete dataset reflects a distorted image of the past. However, this is the case for any other reconstruction based on incomplete sources, regardless of the applied methodology.

The issue of fragmentarily preserved sources is common for the ancient world, but the level of preservation (both in quantity and quality) may differ greatly. For example, if we briefly compare the sites of Assyrian Kaneš (merchant settlement in Asia Minor)[5] and Egyptian Lahun,[6] both flourishing around the XIX–XVIII centuries BC as important political, economic, and cultural settlements, and both producing a large quantity of written sources, some significant differences will be noted. For example, the number of Old Assyrian documents discovered in Kaneš reaches almost 23,000. On the other hand, less than one thousand records originate from Lahun (preserving the largest loot of surviving Middle Kingdom papyri).[7]

A comprehensive prosopographic analysis of individual lives, households, and institutional communities of the inhabitants and the working population of Middle Kingdom Lahun, as attested in written records, is still missing.[8] The site may also be useful for the implementation of SNA methods. On the other hand, many important contributions have been made focussing on the demography and size of Kaneš, as well as on individual archives.[9] Adam Anderson, in his dissertation, has investigated the possibilities of SNA for the corpus of Old Assyrian letters from merchant settlements. The reconstructed network(s) of Assyrian merchants in Kaneš and Aššur was vividly interconnected, and they form a perfect example of a 'small world,' as defined in network theory.[10]

Anderson created several networks (such as epistolary and attestation networks) using various criteria for identifying individuals and calculating parameters. Using Social Network Analysis metrics, he also tried to determine the social structure of the merchant settlement and mark its key figures. However, he rightly stated that SNA offers only a fragmentary picture because it is based on the information contained in the preserved documents. Anderson's work certainly does not provide the reader with definite answers, but indicates numerous previously unnoticed aspects and further avenues of research on this important corpus that should be considered.[11] Documents originating from Lahun are still waiting to be analysed collectively.

Lahun and Kaneš can also be compared on the micro level. Among the Lahun papyri, two sets of household registrations are preserved (UC 31263–31265).[12] Documents, dating from the reign of Sekhemkare (c. 1746–1743 BC), list members (mainly women and children) of three generations of the same family, that of the 'soldier' ($ḥ^3$wtj) Sneferu and his father Hori (probably dead at the time when UC 31263 was drawn up).[13] These documents were "found together, rolled up and sealed."[14] Whether they were held privately or in an administrative bureau, they most likely formed a family archive. The three documents mentioning Sneferu additionally record some individuals not belonging to his household – officials in charge of issuing the documents. When the family of Sneferu is situated within the network of persons attested in texts, the created graph displays 70 individuals (i.e., nodes), and 674 relationships (i.e., edges).

The family archive of the merchant Šalim-Aššur and his sons, approximately one century older than the documents mentioning the household of Sneferu, records c. 12,000 tablets found in situ and testifies to six generations of a single family (c. 1932–1869 BC). The Šalim-Aššur network displays 1,075 nodes and 6,891 edges, reflecting the complexity of family and business life, from commercial partnerships to marriage contracts.[15]

Unfortunately, neither Lahun nor any other ancient Egyptian site has revealed a comparable personal archive.

As already noted by Chollier, chronology is another important obstacle.[16] In social sciences, network analysis is focused on human relations at a specific moment or in a precisely outlined period (in this case, we are dealing with a dynamic network). Would this be possible for any ancient society, including Ancient Egypt? For example, even if we were able to detect, as precisely as possible, three generations of family members on a certain object – we may name it 'stela X' – we could not be sure whether the given monument reflects a time span of c. 105 years (given the time span of 35 years for a generation), or 70 years, or 35 years. We do not know whether 'person A,' in a certain moment of his/her life, mentions his/her parents (and their generation) and grandparents (and their generation), because they are still alive and participate in the commissioning of the ex-voto, or whether they are just named as distinguished past family members. Do we need dead people in the network? Furthermore, how shall we chronologically correlate any individual attested on our 'stela X' with other objects assigned to his/her individual networks?

However, the aforementioned obstacles and limitations are not restricted to network approaches and can raise questions in any other historical or archaeological method, or for any Classical or Ancient Near Eastern discipline.

Not every theory, methodology, and/or approach is applicable to every study, and while there are obvious disadvantages to conducting network research on ancient Egyptian data, there are also some advantages (visualisation being one of the most important).

Christian Rollinger recently formulated some essential questions that need to be answered when applying a network approach:

What criteria were used in the construction of the network? Which actors and what types of connections and relationships do the intricate (and often visually overwhelming) network graphs represent? What is their analytical value? What software was used in drawing them up, and what algorithms and software functions were employed to take quantitative measures?[17]

36 Social Network Analysis and Egyptology

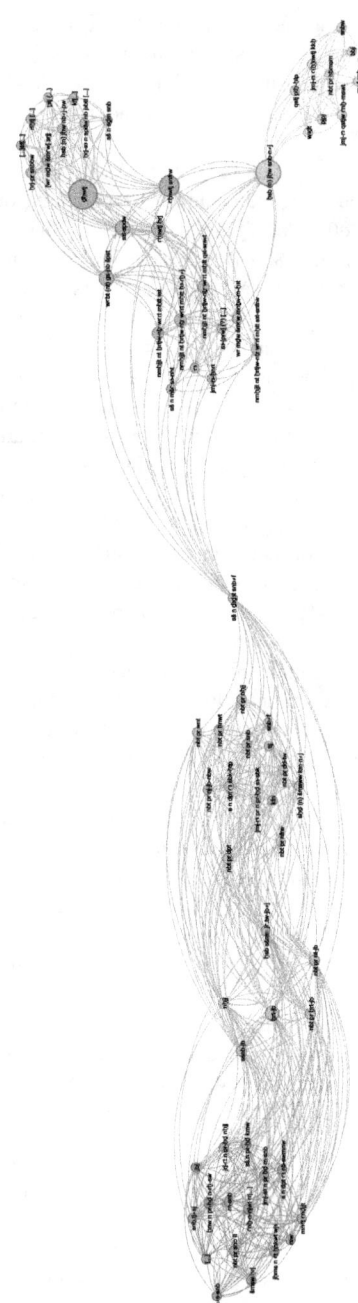

Figure 4.1 The one-mode network of the 'soldier' (ꜥḥwtj) Sneferu

These four questions are equally good starting points for Egyptology.

The first and perhaps the main field in which network theory and SNA can be implemented in Egyptology (and the same is true for almost all disciplines!) is prosopographic research.[18] Indeed, it is not surprising that prosopography, being itself a type of rudimentary network, and Social Network Analysis are 'soul mates'; therefore, most of the projects and published works combine prosopography and SNA. The classical prosopographic charts, or genealogical tables, can exemplify neither the quantity of data (especially relevant for large datasets)[19] nor various layers of their relatedness through one image, as it is possible to present with a single graph (or sociogram).

For prosopographic research in Egyptology, SNA is helpful in overcoming the difficulties caused by our (mis)understanding of ancient Egyptian kinship terms (as exemplified by Chollier).[20] The imprecision of the term 'sn' (literally *brother*), for example, which may refer to any male–male or male–female kin relation, or be used in a more metaphorical sense expressing 'closeness' to a certain individual (as is also the modern usage: to address someone with 'brother'),[21] is highly problematic when we try to reconstruct genealogical charts.

The same is true for lexemes used to define various categories of household members and staff. The size of ancient Egyptian households varied greatly, depending on the individual's social status.[22] Consequently, the ancient Egyptian lexica preserved many terms referring to the relationships of household members, either for nuclear or extended families, including those specifying individuals attached to the household as servants, clients, dependants, or even colleagues. Some of these categories are either difficult to specify or are wrongly rendered.[23] Social Network Analysis greatly helps in overcoming these difficulties. As Chollier stated:

> we do not need to know the real connection between two persons to illustrate it, the existence of the link being the only crucial information. Graphs are less sensitive to link values than genealogical trees. In the latter, the link value between two individuals defines their position in the genealogical tree. In a graph, both of them are represented the same way whatever way they were related.[24]

Indeed, sometimes it is of greater value to recognise the existence of a link between individuals than to be precise as to whether 'person A' is the son of a brother, or the son of a sister, of 'person B.'

However, it needs to be stressed that, taken out of the historical or archaeological context, a network is just a graph providing statistical data, and by itself does not lead anywhere. As stressed by Rollinger, (historical) network research should be "the logical extension of traditional prosopographical research, as prosopography is the only means by which ancient historians interested in social networks may gather enough reliable data," and SNA should "identify and analyse the effect of overarching structural elements of society."[25]

In both prosopography and in datasets created for software (for SNA; to be transferred into *node* and *edge* lists), the identification of an individual is crucial. A name, title, source, and any relevant data providing information about family members will help to establish a stable personal dossier. However, it is not so rare that names and titles are common, with a high number of attestations. For example, the online database "Persons and Names of the Middle Kingdom" (PNM) records twelve individuals, all named 'estate overseer (mr pr) jmnjj,' from an approximately coherent chronological framework (Late Middle Kingdom). They hold a very common title and an even more common name.[26] In the traditional approach, as can be observed in the database interface, they are distinguished by the object that mentions them.

The same can be done by organising data to be analysed by Social Network Analysis. The file created for the software (the author is using Gephi) should include all possible relatedness data: the relationship between individuals and the monuments on which they are attested, interpersonal ties and their nature (family ties and relationships of subordination), professional and status markers (i.e., office and rank titles), and gender.[27]

Visualisation – through graphs or created sociograms – are among the most important advantages of SNA. With the traditional prosopographic approach, be it with genealogical charts or dossiers, the broader picture (no matter how fragmentary it may be in reality) is always missing.

To create a broader picture, the 'snowball sampling method,' also known as chain-referral sampling, may be very useful. This is a non-probability sampling method often used in qualitative research when actors are hard to reach or hidden.[28] How does it work? When we create the ego-network of 'person V,' we look further for the ego-networks of all the individuals attested in his/her initial circle, expanding his/her level of relatedness.

Chollier has shown how the 'snowball sampling' method helped him to reconstruct the network of 'the head of Mêdjayu' Ameneminet, from the reign of Ramesses II (c. 1279–1213 BC). He started with the statue Naples 1069, recording 27 people. Using the snowball sampling method, the network of Ameneminet expanded to 177 connected individuals.[29] Although the "snowball sampling" method may appear to be a never-ending game, Chollier stressed that the chain of enlargement should not go beyond the third link, or zone:

> (1) given the fragmentary aspect of the documentation, a few groups of documents allow deeper research than the third zone; (2) according to an empirical practice, zone 4 does not include new remarkable people; and last, (3) we might consider individuals from the first zone were not so close to those of the third zone; going further would be a kind of abstraction.[30]

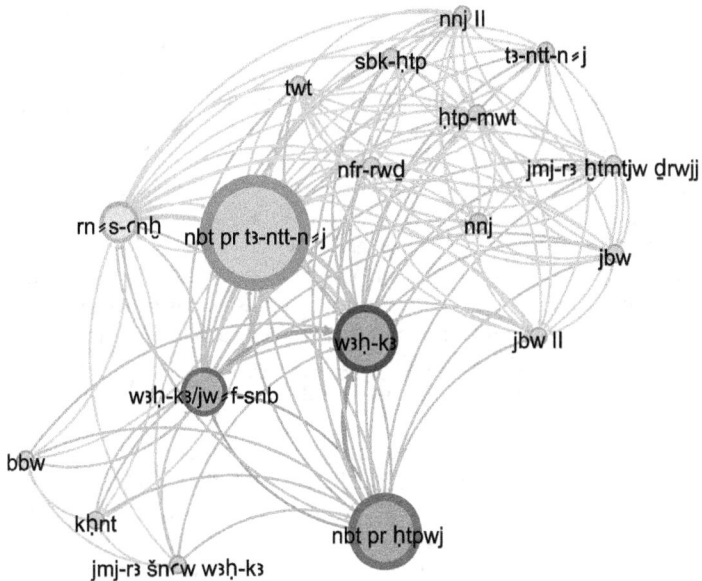

Figure 4.2 The one-mode network of the lady tȝ-ntt-n.j
Compare with Stefanović (2019b), 182–183.

However, alongside the cautious approach rightly advocated by Chollier, reaching farther than 'zone three' may be fruitful for overcoming chronological gaps, more completely outlining generational sequences, and more precisely mapping the 'micro networks' revealed by the analysed datasets.

Prosopography is certainly not the only area in which Egyptology may benefit from network approaches. Giovanni Ruffini has argued that Social Network Analysis could be employed to mark several types of connections: person to person (based on the frequency of attestation in the text, if the exact nature of the connection between two people is known), person to place (special attestation), place to place (special mapping), and person or place to an event, if, according to Ruffini, a person or place is attested in the same source together with other people and places.[31] The ultimate aim of SNA is to determine the existence of clusters of networks of some kind, so the fact that two people are mentioned together in a document as being in the same place, or that two objects originate from the same place, could be sufficient to establish a 'relationship' between them.

While person-to-person connections could be the seed of a study on relatedness, a mere mention is often insufficient, and complementary information would be necessary to ascertain the nature of that relationship. The use of SNA tools on the already recognised informal networks of authority, dependency, micro-social structures, or economic and production units may shed new light or help us to see the data available to us from a new perspective.[32] The material from Deir el-Medina, as this site has produced sufficient inscriptional sources to characterise the community with relative accuracy, could be fruitful for the SNA approach.[33]

Profound studies by Chollier, Martinet, Tambs, Anne Herzberg-Beiersdorf, Dulíková, and Mařík have clearly shown that the various aspects of social transformations, both on the national and provincial level (changes of social structure, mobility, new administrative offices and titles, the appearance of sub-elites, etc.), with the help of visual representations of reconstructed social networks, may provide a more detailed comprehension of the hierarchy between and within the various social groups (including the household members, but also among people who were involved in similar institutions or administrative branches).[34]

The potential of Social Network Analysis for micro-historical research on a larger scale still needs to be explored. For example, the list of workers preserved on the verso of the Late Middle Kingdom/Early Second Intermediate Period (c. 1848–1700 BC) papyrus Brooklyn 35.1446 records 79 servants (male and female Egyptians, Asiatics, and children). They are labelled as 'generous gifts' in the fragmentary letter known as Insert C of papyrus Brooklyn 35.1446, indicating the transfer of a labour population from one estate to another.[35] The procedure involved the vizier Ankhu, the high-ranking official of the central administration. Apart from referring to Ankhu's office, these records also reveal the involvement of his estates and family members.

It has already been noted that some of the individuals recorded on the papyrus Brooklyn 35.1446 are attested on several other monuments, namely on the stelae Cairo CG 20018 and Hermitage 1064, and on the papyrus Boulaq 18 (smaller manuscript).[36] Although around three thousand prosopographic dossiers of ancient Egyptians (both male and female, active during the first half of the II millennia BC, i.e., approximately the period of the Middle Kingdom and Second Intermediate Period) have been established to date, identifying a dependent foreigner or descendent of a dependent foreigner in multiple records is rather rare.

For example, several individuals attested in the above-mentioned records were marked as 'Asiatics' (ancient Egyptian ꜥmw – a general term for west Semitic populations) or descendants of an Asiatic; such are the cases of ꜥmw 'domestic servant' (ḥrj-pr) twtwjt/'nḥw-m-ḥst,[37] 'domestic servant' (ḥrj-pr) rsw/rs-snb,[38] and 'cook' (psjj) snb-nb.f.[39] The two domestic servants (ḥrj-pr), when named in the list of dependents in papyrus Brooklyn 35.1446, are marked as Asiatics, while on stelae their 'ethnonym' is missing. Although

Social Network Analysis and Egyptology 41

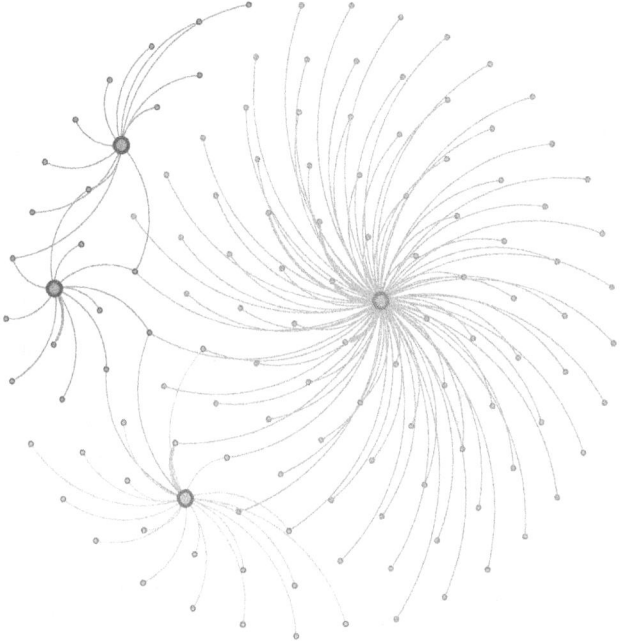

Figure 4.3 Two-mode network of the list of workers preserved on the verso of the late Middle Kingdom papyrus Brooklyn 35.1446 and additional documents

the 'cook' (psjj) snb-nb.f is not identified as Asiatic, he is named on papyrus Brooklyn 35.1446 as the descendent of the Asiatic woman (ꜥmt) hjjbjrw/ nḥ.n.j-m-ḫꜣst.

The rather complex network(s) of high- and medium-ranking Egyptian officials and their staff and servants attested in the above-mentioned records have been profoundly analysed in the works of interested researchers.[40] However, the traditional approach (prosopography and dossiers) cannot provide a complete picture at once. When converted into graphs, the reconstructed network(s) appear as follows:

Certainly, visualisation cannot be the only outcome of historical network research and Social Network Analysis, but a created network, and network theory itself, may allow us to see the analysed data in a new light, raise new questions, or re-evaluate the sources.

Studies by Martinet of provincial elites in Egypt during the VI Dynasty (c. 2345–2181 BC) highlight the interactions between the members of the different social groups through the network approach, such as the case of the

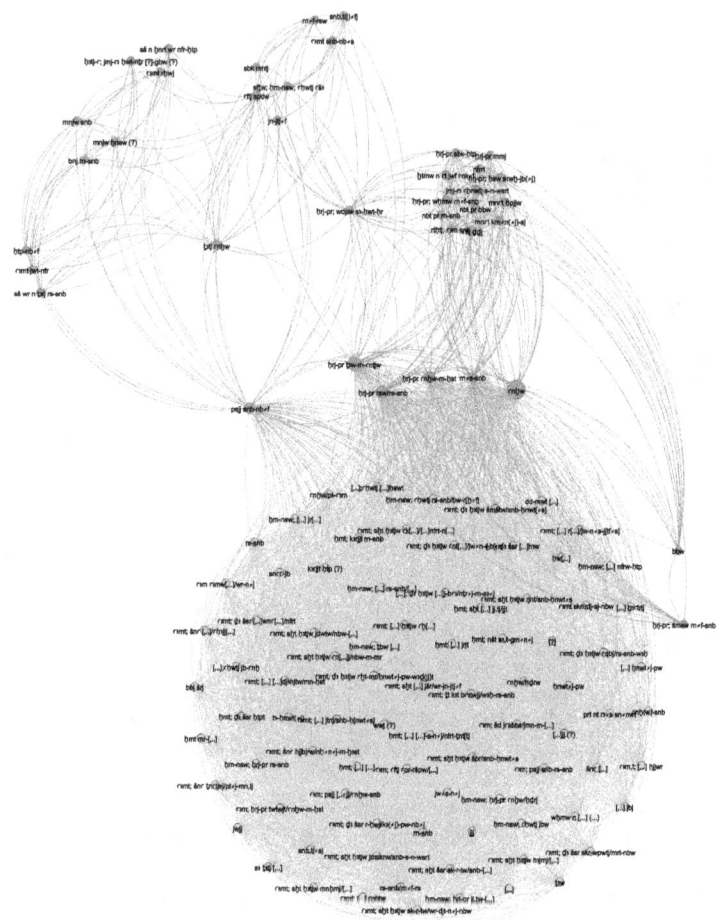

Figure 4.4 One-mode network of the list of workers preserved on the verso of the late Middle Kingdom papyrus Brooklyn 35.1446

high-ranking official Pepyankhheryib.[41] The high-ranking late Old Kingdom individuals analysed by Miroslav Barta, Dulíková, and Mařík exemplify the level of influence a given individual may manifest, and his closeness to the king.[42] In all the aforementioned works, the graphs and visual aspects of the reached conclusions make them more comprehensible than the traditional presentation of the results.

The implementation of SNA methods to studies of household communities, which were basic units of ancient Egyptian social organisation and were frequently multifaceted social networks embracing relatives besides members of nuclear families, serfs, clients, subordinates, and dependants,[43] is another venue still waiting to be more profoundly exploited by the network approach.

The criticisms, most often uttered by scholars (both historians and archaeologists; the same is true of Egyptologists) advocating against working with network theory, is that Social Network Analysis will not bring new results, solve old research puzzles, or produce new findings. And that is true.

Social Network Analysis and network theory offer powerful conceptual and analytical tools that may allow us to reconstruct, study, and quantify past phenomena in formal manners. Furthermore, SNA may reveal further insights into the motives and restrictions of individual behaviour and into levels of political or social engagement that otherwise remain unrecognised, or contribute to the reconstruction of micro–ego-networks (as shown, for example, in Figure 4.2) – the network may 'identify,' through statistical calculations and algorithms, cliques, hubs, or powerful individuals otherwise blurred in sources or archaeological data. The network approach may also help in the reconstruction of certain types of missing data, such as missing parts of trade networks, patterns of distributions of goods,[44] and/or pottery production.

A point of critique must also be stressed. To apply the network approach to the given datasets, substantial knowledge of the analysed topic is required. For reading graphs and creating networks, with all aspects of their incompleteness, we need to be careful about the limitations of the chosen models, and of the statistical results and measurements of the analysed data. Equally important is recognising what the results of the network analysis mean for specific cases and for the broader contexts of our research. As with any other historical or archaeological method applicable to any discipline, including Egyptology, the context is essential.

There is also considerable distrust toward visualisations, which can be manipulated and do not always present, or sometimes even hide, some quantitative and qualitative aspects of the information provided by a text.[45] Neither Egyptology (history, archaeology, or philology) nor any other Classical or Ancient Near Eastern discipline can claim to have a complete set of sources for any given research question or topic. Thus, we are constantly facing the issue of incomplete datasets, and most likely will never be able to reconstruct a mirror of the real-life past.

Whichever method may bring us even a step closer to our envisaged research goals, it should, while considering all limitations and restrictions, be tested, applied, and re-evaluated. When used complementarily to other historical and archaeological methods, the network approach, Social Network Analysis, and visualisation are potentially powerful research tools. As with many other methodological approaches, there are not always definite answers or final conclusions, but rather stimulating and challenging tools for testing what we do know and what we are supposed to know.

Notes

1 See, for example, Cline and Cline (2015); Dulíková and Mařík (2017); Chollier (2019); Herzberg (2019); Dulíková and Bárta (2020); Martinet (2019a); Sacco (2019); Stefanović (2019a); Bárta et al. (2020); Dutrey (2021); Tambs (2022); Herzberg-Beiersdorf (2023).
2 Brughmans et al. (2016), esp. 10–12.
3 Chollier (2019). See also Dulíková and Mařík (2021), 72–82; Herzberg (2020); Martinet (2020a); Tambs (2022), 94–112, 488–510 (providing the most comprehensive present example of the usage of SNA and network(s) theory(es) in Egyptology).
4 For example, the Thesaurus Linguae Aegyptiae (TLA) enumerates more than 100 lexemes for 'snakes,' and just one, although with doubtful meaning, for 'virgin.' See https://thesaurus-linguae-aegyptiae.de/search.
5 The present-day Kültepe, Turkey; see Larsen (2015).
6 Quirke (2005).
7 See *Persons and Names of the Middle Kingdom*, Version 4 (accessed August 2, 2023) https://pnm.uni-mainz.de/inscriptions?geo-filter=all&place=Lahun.
8 The online database *Persons and Names of the Middle Kingdom*, Version 4 (accessed August 2, 2023), records 3,859 individuals. See https://pnm.uni-mainz.de/info.
9 See Bajramovic (2014).
10 Anderson (2017).
11 Anderson (2017).
12 Collier and Quirke (2004), 110–115.
13 Persons and Names of the Middle Kingdom, Version 4 (person 2198; accessed August 17, 2023) https://pnm.uni-mainz.de/person/2198. For the household of Sneferu, see Kóthay (2001), 352–363.
14 Collier and Quirke (2002), vii, x.
15 Anderson (2020).
16 Chollier (2016) and (2019).
17 Rollinger (2020), 26.
18 "Prosopography is a research method for studying a social group by comparing the biographical (sequence of) data of each of its members. Its aim is to understand how the groups operate, without neglecting the singular behavior. Prosopography is based on a precise, documented investigation of each individual in the determined population" (Akoka, et al., 2018, 1). Katharine Keats-Rohan's influential *Prosopography Approaches and Applications: A Handbook on the Practice of Prosopography* (2007) includes two contributions that sought to combine the two approaches.
19 Jauhiainen and Alstola (2022).
20 Chollier (2019).
21 Revez (2003).
22 Moreno García (2012); Picardo (2015) and (2022); Müller (2015).
23 The aforementioned issue especially concerns gender biased lexica and social stratum markers. See Satzinger and Stefanović (2012); Hellum 2020; Stefanović (2024).
24 Chollier (2019), 85–86.
25 Rollinger (2020), 7.

26 The online database *Persons and Names of the Middle Kingdom*, Version 4 (accessed August 16, 2023). See https://pnm.uni-mainz.de/title/4?start=100#inscriptions_id_nav.
27 Chollier (2019), 83–96.
28 See Edwards et al. (1999) and Wasserman and Faust (1994), 84–101.
29 Chollier (2016), 62–63; Chollier (2017) and (2019), 83–96.
30 Chollier (2019), 90–91.
31 Ruffini (2008), 21.
32 See Moreno García (2014).
33 The recently published book by Joanne-Marie Robinson (2020) offers a 'network thinking approach' with regard to the Deir el-Medina material. Unfortunately, not a single graph is included. Network thinking refers to the act of thinking in terms of networks, which does not necessarily involve the application of formal network analysis or network theories to study relational connectivity and the structural composition of network models.
34 Chollier (2016) and (2017); Dulíková and Mařík (2017), (2020) and (2021); Herzberg-Beiersdorf (2023); Martinet (2019a), (2019b), and (2020b); Tambs 2022.
35 Hayes (1955), 105–107; Quirke (1990), 145–146; Mourad (2015), 116-117; Ilin-Tomich (2021).
36 Franke (1984), 248, 537, 386; Grajetzki and Stefanović (2012), 229; Ilin-Tomich (2021), 153–157.
37 Franke (1984), 183. See also Persons and Names of the Middle Kingdom, Version 4 (person 183; accessed August 2, 2023) https://pnm.uni-mainz.de/person/183.
38 Persons and Names of the Middle Kingdom, Version 4 (person 2159; accessed August 2, 2023) https://pnm.uni-mainz.de/person/2159.
39 Persons and Names of the Middle Kingdom, Version 4 (person 2158; accessed August 2, 2023) https://pnm.uni-mainz.de/person/2158.
40 For an extensive overview, see Ilin-Tomich (2021).
41 Martinet (2020b).
42 Bárta et al. (2020); Dulíková and Mařík (2017).
43 Moreno García (2012) and (2013), 1050; see also Martinet (2020a), 72; Moreno García (2020).
44 See, for example Sacco (2019).
45 Düring and Kerschbaumer (2016), 39; see also Staley (2014), 53–61; Broux and Pietowski (2020), 156.

References

Akoka, J., Comyn-Wattiau, I., Lamassé, S., & Du Mouza, C. (2018). Conceptual modelling of prosopographic databases integrating quality dimensions. *Journal of Data Mining and Digital Humanities: Special Issue on Data Science and Digital Humanities*. https://doi.org/10.46298/jdmdh.5078. HAL Id: hal-01966374v5

Anderson, A. (2017). *The Old Assyrian social network: An analysis of the texts from Kültepe Kanesh (1950–1750 B.C.E.)* [Unpublished doctoral dissertation]. Harvard University.

Bajramovic, G. (2014). The size of Kanesh and the demography of early middle bronze age Anatolia. In L. Atici, F. Kulakoğlu, G. Barjamovic, & A. Fairbairn (Eds.), *Current research in Kültepe/Kanesh: An interdisciplinary and integrative approach to trade networks, internationalism, and identity during the middle bronze age* (pp. 55–68). Lockwood Press. https://doi.org/10.2307/j.ctvvnd58.6

Bárta, M., Dulíková, V., Mařík, R., & Cibuľa, M. (2020). Modelling the dynamics of ancient Egyptian state during the Old Kingdom period: Hidden Markov Models and social network analysis. *Zeitschrift für Ägyptische Sprache und Altertumskunde, 149*(1), 1–16. https://doi.org/10.1515/zaes-2020-0017

Broux, Y., & Pietowski, F. (2020). Trismegistos' TOMATILLO: A new tool to visualize related data in an online environment. In M. Barta & V. Dulikova (Eds.), *Addressing the dynamics of change in ancient Egypt: Complex network analysis* (pp. 154–170). Charles University in Prague.

Brughmans, T., Collar, A., & Coward, F. (Eds.). (2016). *The connected past: Challenges to network studies in archaeology and history*. Oxford University Press. https://doi.org/10.1093/oso/9780198748519.001.0001

Chollier, V. (2016). Analyse des réseaux d'élites en Égypte ancienne. Réflexions sur des solutions méthodologiques. In R. Letricot, M. Cuxac, M. Uzcategui, & A. Cavaletto (Eds.), *Le réseau. Usages d'une notion polysémique en sciences humaines et sociales* (pp. 57–72). Presses universitaires de Louvain.

Chollier, V. (2017). *Administrer les cultes au Nouvel Empire (1539-1077 av. J.-C.): stratégies sociales et territoriales* [Unpublished doctoral dissertation]. Université de Lyon.

Chollier, V. (2019). Social network analysis in Egyptology: Benefits, methods and limits. *Journal of Egyptian Archaeology, 105*, 83–96. https://doi.org/10.1177/0307513319889329

Cline, D. H., & Cline, E. H. (2015). Text messages, tablets, and social networks: The "small world" of the Amarna letters. In J. Mynářová, P. Onderka, & P. Pavúk (Eds.), *There and back again – The crossroads II* (pp. 17–44). Charles University in Prague.

Collier, M., & Quirke, S. (2002). *The UCL Lahun papyri: Letters*. Archaeopress.

Collier, M., & Quirke, S. (2004). *The UCL Lahun papyri: Religious, literary, legal, mathematical and medical*. Archaeopress.

Dulíková, V., & Bárta, M. (Eds.). (2020). *Addressing the dynamics of change in ancient Egypt: Complex network analysis*. Charles University in Prague.

Dulíková, V., & Mařík, R. (2017). Complex network analysis in Old Kingdom society: A nepotism case. In M. Bárta, F. Coppens, & J. Krejčí (Eds.), *Abusir and Saqqara in the year 2015* (pp. 63–83). Prague.

Dulíková, V., & Mařík, R. (2020). Cyber-Egyptology: An overview of tools: Cybernetics, artificial intelligence, complex networks. In M. Barta & V. Dulikova (Eds.), *Addressing the dynamics of change in ancient Egypt: Complex network analysis* (pp. 29–70). Charles University in Prague.

Dulíková, V., & Mařík, R. (2021). Uncovering Old Kingdom society arrangement: Detection of powerful dignitaries using complex network analysis. In C. Gracia Zamacona & J. Ortiz-García (Eds.), *Handbook of digital Egyptology: Texts* (pp. 69–102). Universidad de Alcalá.

Düring, M., & Kerschbaumer, F. (2016). Quantifizierung und Visualisierug, Anknüpfungspunkte in den Geschichtswissenschaften. In M. Düring, U. Eumann, M. Stark, & L. von Keyserlingkeds (Eds.), *Handbuch Historische Netzwerkforschung: Grundlagen und Anwendungen* (pp. 31–42). LIT Verlag.

Dutrey, C. (2021). Distribution de l'information et stratégies relationnelles dans le corpus de correspondances amarniennes: approche par l'analyse de réseaux. *Journal of Historical Network Research, 6*(1). https://doi.org/10.25517/jhnr.v6i1.85

Edwards, R., Ribbens, J., & Gillies, V. (1999). Shifting boundaries and power in the research process: The example of researching 'step-families'. In J. Seymour & P. Bagguley (Eds.), *Relating intimacies: Power and resistance* (pp. 13–42). Palgrave Macmillan. https://doi.org/10.1007/978-1-349-27683-7_2

Franke, D. (1984). *Personendaten aus dem Mittleren Reich (20.–16. Jahrhundert v. Chr.): Dossiers 1–796*. Otto Harrassowitz.

Grajetzki, W., & Stefanović, D. (2012). *Dossiers of ancient Egyptians – The Middle Kingdom and second intermediate period: Addition to Franke's "Personendaten."* Golden House Publications.

Hayes, W. C. (1955). *A papyrus of the late Middle Kingdom in the Brooklyn Museum*. Brooklyn Museum.

Hellum, J. (2020). The questions of the maidservant and the concubine: Re-examining Egyptian female lexicology. In A. R. Warfe, J. C. R. Gill, C. R. Hamilton, A. J. Pettman, & D. A. Stewart (Eds.), *Dust, demons and pots: Studies in honour of Colin A. Hope* (pp. 269–278). Peeters Publishers. https://doi.org/10.2307/j.ctv1q26ngg.27

Herzberg, A. (2019). Prosopographia Memphitica – Analyzing prosopographical data and personal networks from the Memphite necropolis. In N. Staring, H. Twiston Davies, & L. Weiss (Eds.), *Perspectives on lived religion: Practices – Transmission – Landscape* (pp. 39–58). Sidestone Press.

Herzberg, A. (2020). Towards a memphite prosopography of the new Kingdom – Promises and pitfalls of historical network analysis. In M. Barta & V. Dulikova (Eds.), *Addressing the dynamics of change in ancient Egypt: Complex network analysis* (pp. 105–136). Charles University in Prague.

Herzberg-Beiersdorf, A. (2023). *Prosopographia Memphitica. Individuelle Identitäten und kollektive Biographien einer königlichen Residenzstadt des Neuen Reichs*. De Gruyter. https://doi.org/10.1515/9783110783650

Ilin-Tomich, A. (2021). The Vizier Ankhu and the dual vizierate in the late Middle Kingdom. *Journal of Egyptian History*, *14*(2), 145–169. https://doi.org/10.1163/18741665-12340075

Jauhiainen, H., & Alstola, T. (2022). A social network of the prosopography of the Neo-Assyrian empire. *Journal of Open Humanities Data*, *8*, 8. https://doi.org/10.5334/johd.74

Keats-Rohan, K. (Ed.). (2007). *Prosopography approaches and applications: A handbook*. University of Oxford.

Kóthay, K. A. (2001). Houses and households at Kahun: Bureaucratic and domestic aspects of social organisation during the Middle Kingdom. In H. Győry (Ed.), *Mélanges offerts à Edith Varga: le lotus qui sort de terre, Bulletin du Musée Hongrois des Beaux-Arts Suppl* (pp. 349–368). Musée Hongrois des Beaux-Arts.

Larsen, M. T. (2015). *Ancient Kanesh: A merchant colony in bronze age Anatolia*. Cambridge University Press. https://doi.org/10.1017/CBO9781316344781

Martinet, É. (2019a). *L'Administration provinciale sous l'Ancien Empire égyptien*. Brill. https://doi.org/10.1163/9789004407190

Martinet, É. (2019b). Social differentiation and degree of integration in court society: Towards sociology of the provincial elites in the old kingdom. In A. Delli Castelli & P. Piacentini (Eds.), *EDAL VI: Paper presented to the OKAA 7th Conference, Milano, July 7, 2017* (pp. 260–273). Pontremoli Editore.

Martinet, É. (2020a). Pratique de la Social Network Analysis en égyptologie et apports à l'étude des réseaux de relations des élites en Égypte ancienne. *Claroscuro, 19*(2), 1–28. http://hdl.handle.net/2133/20309

Martinet, É. (2020b). Analysing the dynamics among the social groups and the mechanisms of social promotion in the provinces in the late Old Kingdom: SNA Methods and new research approaches. In M. Barta & V. Dulikova (Eds.), *Addressing the dynamics of change in ancient Egypt: Complex network analysis* (pp. 71–95). Charles University in Prague.

Moreno García, J. C. (2012). Households. In E. Frood & W. Wendrich (Eds.), *UCLA Encyclopedia of Egyptology*, Los Angeles. http://digital2.library.ucla.edu/viewItem.do?ark=21198/zz002czx07

Moreno García, J. C. (2013). The 'other' administration. Patronage, factions, and informal networks of power in ancient Egypt. In J. C. Moreno García (Ed.), *Ancient Egyptian administration* (pp. 1029–1065). Brill. https://doi.org/10.1163/9789004250086_023

Moreno García, J. C. (2014). Recent developments in the social and economic history of ancient Egypt. *Journal of Ancient Near Eastern History, 1*(2), 231–261. https://doi.org/10.1515/janeh-2014-0002

Moreno García, J. C. (2020). Clientele, power and family bonds in ancient Egypt: Building social links, promoting individual strategies, facing kin conflicts. *Soziale Systeme, 25*(1), 30–60. https://doi.org/10.1515/sosys-2020-0002

Mourad, A.-L. (2015). *Rise of the Hyksos: Egypt and the levant from the Middle Kingdom to the early second intermediate period*. Archaeopress. https://doi.org/10.2307/j.ctvr43jbk

Müller, M. (2015). New approaches to the study of households in Middle Kingdom and second intermediate period Egypt. In M. Müller (Ed.), *Household studies in complex societies. (Micro) archaeological and textual approaches* (pp. 237–255). The Oriental Institute of the University of Chicago.

Picardo, N. (2015). Hybrid households: Institutional affiliations and household identity in the town of Wah-sut (South Abydos). In M. Müller (Ed.), *Household studies in complex societies. (Micro) archaeological and textual approaches* (pp. 243–287). The Oriental Institute of the University of Chicago.

Picardo, N. (2022). 'Social house' theory and Egyptian archaeology. In L. Battini, A. Brody, & S. R. Steadman (Eds.), *No place like home: Ancient near eastern houses and households* (pp. 6–20). Archaeopress.

Quirke, S. (1990). *The administration of Egypt in the late Middle Kingdom: The hieratic documents*. SIA Publications.

Quirke, S. (2005). *Lahun: A town in Egypt 1800 BC, and the history of its landscape*. Golden House Publications.

Revez, J. (2003). The metaphorical use of the kinship term sn "brother". *Journal of the American Research Center in Egypt, 40*, 123–131. https://doi.org/10.2307/40000295

Robinson, J.-M. (2020). *'Blood Is Thicker Than Water': Non-royal consanguineous marriage in ancient Egypt. An exploration of economic and biological outcomes*. Archaeopress. https://doi.org/10.2307/j.ctv15vwjpj

Rollinger, C. (2020). Prolegomena. Problems and perspectives of historical network research and ancient history. *Journal of Historical Network Research, 4*, 1–35. https://doi.org/10.25517/jhnr.v4i0.72

Ruffini, G. R. (2008). *Social networks in Byzantine Egypt*. Cambridge University Press. https://doi.org/10.1017/CBO9780511552014

Sacco, A. (2019). Game of dots: Using network analysis to examine the regionalization in the second intermediate period. In M. Bietak & S. Prell (Eds.), *The enigma of the Hyksos: Volume I* (pp. 369–396). Harrassowitz Verlag. https://doi.org/10.13173/9783447113328

Satzinger, H., & Stefanović, D. (2012). The Middle Kingdom ḥnmsw. *Studien zur altägyptischen Kultur*, *41*, 341–351. http://www.jstor.org/stable/41812232

Staley, D. J. (2014). *Computers, visualisation, and history: How new technology will transform our understanding of the past*. Routledge.

Stefanović, D. (2019a). The social network(s) of the Middle Kingdom and second intermediate period treasurers: Rehuerdjersen, Siese, Ikhernefret and Senebsumai. *Journal of Egyptian History*, *12*, 259–287. https://doi.org/10.1163/18741665-12340054

Stefanović, D. (2019b). Varia Epigraphica VI: The Middle Kingdom. *Göttinger Miszellen. Beiträge zur ägyptologischen Diskussion*, *257*, 177–185.

Stefanović, D. (2024). The way to behave to a man's ḥbswt is known. *Bulletin of the Egyptological Seminar, 2024* (forthcoming).

Tambs, L. (2022). *Socio-economic relations in ptolemaic pathyris: A network analytical approach to a bilingual community*. Brill. https://doi.org/10.1163/9789004500266

Wasserman, S., & Faust, K. (1994). *Social network analysis: Methods and applications*. Cambridge University Press. https://doi.org/10.1017/CBO9780511815478

5 'The small world of the Abydos votive zone' – the game of graphs, glyphs, and objects

> Abydos appears once to have been a great city, second only to Thebes, but it is now only a small settlement.
>
> (Strabo, *Geography*, 17.1.42)

5.1 Setting a scene

The ancient Abydos (ancient Egyptian ꜣbḏw, later Ebōt in Coptic), comprising the modern-day villages of el-'Araba el-Madfuna, Beni Mansur, and Deir Sitt Damyana, lies about 500km south of Cairo, in Upper Egypt, on the west bank of the Nile, in the modern province of Sohag. The site, which extends over 8km², is located approximately 13km west of the Nile River. During the dynastic period, Abydos geographically belonged to Thinite Nome. Over the course of nearly four millennia, the site was home to temples, cemeteries, and several towns and villages. As a necropolis, Abydos was used during the entire timeline of ancient Egypt, from the Predynastic to the Christian eras.

The site of Abydos, rediscovered to Western scholarship by Claude Sicard in 1718, is archaeologically rich, and diverse aspects of its complex materiality have been studied and published in varying degrees of detail since the XIX century. The first wave of excavation at the site occurred between the 1850s and the 1920s, and the second wave began in 1967 and continues to the present day.[1]

The area of Abydos can be divided into two main locations according to the geographic features of the site: North Abydos and South Abydos. North Abydos includes the Osiris Temple and town site, the Cultic Zone, the Middle and North cemeteries, and the Early Dynastic Enclosures. South Abydos was the home of the large Late Middle Kingdom town of Wah-sut-Kha-kau-Re-Maa-Kheru-em-Abdju (Wah-sut) – "Enduring are the places of Khakaure, True of voice, in Abydos" – a mortuary temple dedicated to the memory of Senwosret III (c. 1878–1839 BC), and of at least three royal tombs.[2]

The prominence of Abydos grew over time, and was caused by several factors. The tombs of some of the first kings of unified Egypt were built there

DOI: 10.4324/9781003457015-5

(i.e., in Umm el-Qa'āb). At the site, these early kings also built funerary enclosures that were, perhaps, counterparts to their tombs in Umm el-Qa'ab. These constructions were probably at the same time locations of cultic activities on behalf of the deceased king.

The importance of Abydos was also rooted in its cultic landscape.[3] A deity initially worshiped at the site was the local canid god Khentiamentiu ("Foremost of the Westerners") who, in addition to being charged with the protection of the Abydene cemeteries, was the object of the local cult. Towards the late Old Kingdom (c. 2686–2181 BC) Khentiamentiu became assimilated with Osiris, the god of the underworld and resurrection, who was strongly identified with Abydos in the Pyramid Texts and was thereafter also worshipped at the site.

The cult of Osiris was an important element of ancient Egyptian royal dogma. Egyptians believed that when the king died, he journeyed to the underworld and became one with the god Osiris, the ruler of the afterlife. Perhaps as a result of the cults of the dead kings buried at Abydos, the site itself became one of the primary locations for the worship of Osiris and his connection with the afterlife. The legitimacy of kingship and the Osiride transformation of the deceased king marked Abydos as a site of great importance.

For ancient Egyptians, the ruler was a semi-divine being, a link between the world of the gods and the world of humans, and the importance of Abydos as a religious centre grew steadily through Egyptian history. As time progressed, the Egyptian kings and commoners endeavoured to connect their funerary cults with the temple of Osiris at Abydos and the rituals associated with his worship.

During the Middle Kingdom (c. 2040–1750 BC) the site of Abydos was one of the most prominent places in the Nile valley, as the centre of cult for the god Osiris-Khentiamentiu and the site of his major temple. Josef Wegner attributed the growth of Abydos' prominence in the XII Dynasty to the formalisation of the Osiris cult and its close association with kingship.[4] Consequently, the importance of Abydos as a cult centre worth of royal patronage and as the place of growing non-royal funerary cultic activity reaches a new height.

By the end of the III millennium, as far as it can be traced in sources, ancient Egyptians began to believe that the final resting place of Osiris was located at Abydos at the site of the Early Dynastic royal tombs in Um el-Qa'āb: the tomb of I Dynasty King Djer (c. 3000 BC) was identified as a tomb of the god Osiris.[5] At some point, this belief was transformed into a yearly festival, re-enacting the events from the Osiris myth, commemorating his life, death, rebirth, and his realm in the underworld (in reality connecting early Dynastic tombs, Osiris, and the Osiris temple).[6] During the festival, the statue of Osiris was ritually paraded out of the temple, processed up the wadi leading to his 'tomb' at Umm el-Qa'āb, and then returned to the temple.[7]

The growing prominence of the site also became attractive to the common people. Consequently, worshippers gathered in Abydos for the Osiris festival. People could participate by standing along the processional route to witness the god passing by, or attend transcendentally by constructing votive chapels along and near the route, thereby not only magically partaking in the ceremony, but also linking their fates to that of Osiris, hoping to become one with the god in the afterlife.[8] Pilgrims also used to leave offerings to the god in the form of small pots, which are now so numerous that the local Arabic name for the area became Umm el Qa'āb, that is "mother of pots."

As previously mentioned, the physical presence of individuals was not the only possible means of being close to the deity. Over the course of the Middle Kingdom, non-royal individuals commissioned stelae and other portable objects (statues, offering tables etc.) to be installed in the offering chapels constructed at the site.[9] These chapels were built outside the Osiris Temple enclosure in northern Abydos, at a site called rwd n nṯr ^{q} – "the Terrace of the Great God."[10]

This votive zone, extending along the processional route and overlooking the Osiris temple, allowed Egyptians who built chapels there to 'view' the procession symbolically, to take part in the ceremony, to maintain the memory of a group to which they have belonged, and to benefit from the god's blessings in perpetuity.[11] Chapels were oriented north-east towards the Osiris temple, the starting point of the Neshmet barque procession to Poqer (modern Umm el-Qa'āb and the location of the first royal cemetery in dynastic history). At the end of the festival, this was the last point at which the resurrected god was visible before entering his temple.[12]

Although some of the chapels were commissioned by kings, the vast majority were built by non-royal people originating from various strata of society: from high-ranking dignitaries and members of the elite, to modest local artisans and commoners.[13] For example, the stela of the 'estate overseer' (mr pr) Dediqu (Berlin 1199), reports how he was passing through Abydos after an official venture, commissioned a stela, and dedicated a new chapel with offerings before he continued on his way home.[14]

The number of chapels constructed within the votive zone cannot be determined with certainty.[15] However, the area of the Terrace of the Great God, as stated by J. Wegner, "has produced the largest concentration of private stelae – more than one thousand examples – from any Middle Kingdom site."[16] Consequently, the objects from Abydos "are the single largest and most important source of personal information, including identities and occupations, on 'sub-elite' ('middle class') Egyptians of the Middle Kingdom, and possibly of any other period."[17]

William Kelly Simpson's publication *The Terrace of the Great God at Abydos: The Offering Chapels of Dynasties 12 and 13*, technically introduced the concept of 'Abydos North Offering Chapel (ANOC)' groups, trying to establish links between individual artefacts (stelae, statues, blocks, and/or offering tables), or assemblages of pieces, and clusters.[18] The objects were brought together based on several criteria: prosopographic data, iconography, epigraphy, chronological phases of chapel building, or workshop attributions. The idea of the existence of chapels was postulated based on several mudbrick structures excavated by David O'Connor in the 1970s.[19] Simpson initially proposed the existence of 78 ANOC assemblages.[20]

Over the years, the corpus of ANOC clusters has been modified by several researchers, either by adding new objects, or by disputing the assemblages established by Simpson.[21] Abdel-Méguid El-Rabi'i supplemented the original ANOC list with the significant addition of 29 extra groups.[22] Most recently Leire Olabarria compiled all the suggested corrections and assembled a list comprising approximately 300 objects clustered into 109 ANOC groups.[23]

Although there can be many *pro et contra* arguments for the idea of assigning the individual artefacts to clusters, especially due to the fact that provenance for many Abydos objects (including stelae), presently scattered around the world, has not been recorded, and that not so many of them have been discovered in situ,[24] several inscriptions on stelae refer to these chapels as mꜥḥꜥt, specifying that they were built in the place of the rwd n nṯr ꜥ – the 'Terrace of the Great God.'[25] The stela Cairo GC 20099, excavated at Abydos, notes:

> I have made [a mꜥḥꜥt] at the [T]errace of the [G]reat [G]od, lord of life, foremost of Abydos, in the midst of my fathers who created [me?], the nobles of the first occasion, so that [I] may receive offerings in the presence of the great god, and that I may inhale incense...[26]

Furthermore, the inscription of the mꜥḥꜥt formula, attested on the stela London BM 575 likely originating from Abydos, reads:

> I made this [mꜥḥꜥt] at the [T]errace of the [G]reat [G]od, lord of life, foremost of Abydos, so that I may receive offerings, incense, and divine offerings on the offering tables of the lord of the gods, and that there may be said to me, "Welcome," by the great ones of Abydos, and that there be given to me hands in the [Neshmet]-barque on the festivals of the necropolis, and that I receive pure offerings which come forth in the presence of the Great God, after his ka is satisfied therewith, on his good and pure roads which are in the necropolis, and that I might hear the jubilation at the door of Ta-wer on the wonderful night of Haker...[27]

However, it must be noted that although the term mꜥḥꜥt has been used to denote different types of buildings, those constructed in North Abydos are offering chapels whose builders and benefactors were buried elsewhere.[28]

Over the years, various aspects of the ANOC groups have been in the focus of many researchers. Many of the individual ANOC objects, as well as some of the clusters, and their owners have been addressed in analyses of style and workshops, language, titles, kin groups, prosopography and iconography. As the most general observation, it can be noted that individuals from various social, institutional, and economic backgrounds were able to construct a memorial chapel in this area, as evidenced by the differing sizes and quality of the chapels and objects, as well as by the titles and status markers of the persons associated with them. However, a list of persons attested on the objects coming from the votive zone, either assigned to the clusters or not, has never been created (to the best of the author's knowledge). Consequently, as stated by Anne Herzberg regarding the Memphite necropolis, but also of relevance for Abydos, "the investigation of the complex system of relational patterns was inevitably concentrated on only a small number of social actors selected by their particular importance."[29] At present, prosopographic research and compiled personal data represent only a very small percentage of the estimated total amount of the 'social capital'[30] of the Abydos votive zone.

Therefore, new approaches to the regional prosopography of the Abydos votive zone are feasible.[31] Leire Olabarria pointed out that ANOC groups should be considered as "hypothetical reconstructions of foci of memory, since their function was to commemorate together certain groups of people, many of whom might have formed kin groups."[32] Indeed, some chapels, or several objects within the chapel, commemorate various groups of individuals. For some groupings the reasons are obvious from the texts: members of kin groups, household personnel, collegial or institutional subordinate networks, and patron–clientelist hubs. Whatever the reason for gathering persons in an mʿḥʿt, every ANOC chapel can perhaps be considered as a hypothetical community binding the individuals attested on the assigned objects. Consequently, if there is a community, there is a prosopography and network(s).

As already indicated, objects placed in memorial chapels in Abydos may belong to family members, relatives, colleagues, or dependants of the owner, or higher-ranking official or *pater familias*.[33] The size of clusters may vary, and sometimes large and small chapels would form a group where smaller chapels may have belonged to relatives, colleagues, or dependants of the owners of the larger ones.[34] In some cases, the nature of a relationship is indicated either by kinship terms (although the meaning of some of them is not always precise – for example *sn*, literally *brother*, may be used for a wide range of family ties, but also metaphorically reflecting patronage),[35] a specific task a group of individuals was engaged to perform, or the hierarchical structure of the institution to which they had been attached. However, very often it is difficult to ascertain the nature of the relationship, or the reason for 'bringing together rather diverse people on a single object,' and in such cases the network approach and Social Network Analysis may help in overcoming the shortage or impreciseness of the available data.[36]

'The small world of the Abydos votive zone' 55

When, for example, several females with the not very revealing title 'mistress of the house' (nbt pr), and without any further specificities, are recorded on the stela of 'a person X,' the only conclusion we can reach is that there 'should be' some sort of connection, otherwise they would not be mentioned on the object. Olabarria rightly states that the function of Abydos stelae should be understood within the unique context of the site itself, "where individuals sought eternal participation in the festivities of Osiris for themselves and for their acquaintances," as well as that they should be approached contextually both as an element of the cluster and the ritual landscape of Abydos.[37]

Indeed, ANOC clusters should only include objects from Abydos. However, in most cases, this is not enough for reconstructing family networks, kin groups, and institutional patterns. Many of the individuals mentioned on the objects from Abydos are also attested on monuments originating from other sites. Although this may appear as a restraining aspect – bearing in mind the network approach, and that humans are not part of one, but of many networks, and that networks are constantly shifting, expanding, overlapping, and finally converging with society itself – the initial obstacle can perhaps be transformed into an advantage. A few examples will follow.

5.2 The treasurer Ikhernefret and ANOC 1

The cluster ANOC 1 most likely consisted of a large chapel surrounded by several associated smaller ones. Eleven objects have been assigned to ANOC 1: Berlin 1204, CGC 20038, CGC 20140, CGC 20310, CGC 20683, London BM EA 202, Louvre C 5, Basel III 5002, Geneva D 50, Louvre C 33, and CGC 20065.[38] More than ten dossiers of individuals attested on given objects are recognised by researchers.[39]

The most prominent person in the ANOC 1 cluster is the 'treasurer' (mr ḫtmt) Ikhernefret (jj-ḫr-nfrt) who served under Senusret III-Amenemhet III.[40] He is attested on stelae commissioned by him and by his subordinates. Except the stela Sinai 83, all other objects belong to his chapel(s) in Abydos. The second most prominent individual in the group is the 'interior-overseer of the bureau of the treasurer' (mr ʿḫnwtj n ḫ³ n mr ḫtmt) s³-stt.[41] It is significant to mention that ANOC 1 is the first large Middle Kingdom assemblage of stelae from Abydos relating to a 'treasurer;' that, perhaps, would be an indication of the growing importance of the treasurer's office during the late Middle Kingdom.

During the Middle Kingdom the mr ḫtmt – 'overseer of sealed things,' or 'treasurer' – was one of the most important officials of the central (court) administration. He was in charge of the palace as an economic unit, responsible for incoming goods, their storage, and the consequent distribution of commodities from the palace. The revenues coming to the residence from all around the country, including raw materials, were also under his control, as well as the royal building projects. [42]

The large number of stelae set up for Ikhernefret and his subordinates at Abydos was connected with his own ventures at that place, correlating with the activities of Senusret III, as especially exemplified in the texts recorded on the stelae Berlin 1204 and Geneva D50. The stela Berlin 1204 specifies royal endeavours (the extensive refurbishment of the Osiris temple and voyage to Nubia) stressing the role Ikhernefret may have played.[43] The inscription reads:

> I conducted the procession of Wep-wawet when he proceeds to avenge his Father. I repelled the rebels from the Neshmet barque and I felled the enemies of Osiris. I conducted the great procession following the god at his footsteps. I caused the god's barque to sail on, with Thoth leading the voyage. I equipped the barque "The lord of Abydos arises in Maat" with a shrine, / his fine regalia being set in place as he proceeded to Poqer in the Thinite Nome. I cleared the god's paths to his cenotaph tomb in front of Poqer. I avenged Wen-nofer on that day of the great fighting, and I felled all his enemies on the sand-banks of Nedit.
> And I had him proceed within the Great Barque and it carried his beauty, gladdening the eastern deserts and [creating] joy in the heart of the western deserts when they saw the beauties of the Neshmet barque as it put to land at Abydos and as it brought back [Osiris-Foremost-of-the-Westerners, Lord] of Abydos to his palace.
> And I followed the god into his temple, his purification done, his throne widened.[44]

The sources mentioning the treasurer Ikhernefret reveal four networks to which he belonged.[45] The one encompassing his family and household members (?) is the weakest. The only firmly attested relative is his mother sꜣt-ḥnsw.[46]

The second network of Ikhernefret is his ego-network (see Figure 5.2), encompassing individuals attested on the objects mentioning him. This group exceeds the ANOC 1. The one-mode ego-network of Ikhernefret consists of 73 nodes (individuals attested on twelve objects) and 585 links (assuming that persons attested on the same object must be somehow connected). The maximum path length (also called geodesic distance or diameter) is 3, and the average path length is 1.466.

Ikhernefret also belongs to the network of the 'community of ANOC 1' (see Figure 5.1) encompassing eleven objects with 112 individuals and 1,524 edges (with caution, as the number is most probably not definite).[47] In this case the maximum path length of the network is 6, and the average path length is 2.628. The average clustering coefficient of the network is 0.478. Ikhernefret lost his central position compared with his ego-network; the clustering coefficient of his node is 0.0118.

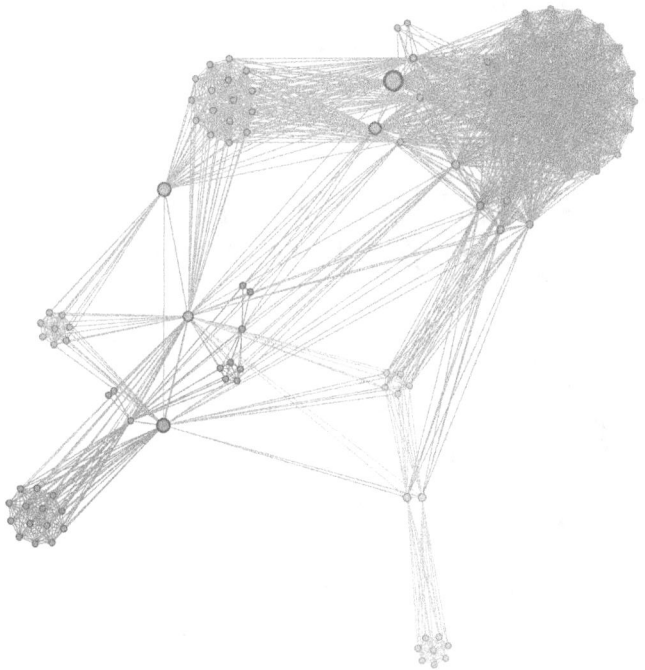

Figure 5.1 The one-mode network of ANOC 1

As already mentioned, some of the individuals from Ikhernefret's world have been attested on additional objects and had their own networks.[48] By using the snow ball sampling method, the modelled network of Ikhernefret gradually expanded, and the two types of graphs possible using the Gephi software were created. The two-mode network graph, linking the objects and persons, has 628 nodes linked with 701 edges (see Figure 5.3). After collapsing the bipartite to a monopartite network, the macro network of 563 nodes, grouped in 11 clusters and 8,840 edges, is modelled; the score for the average local clustering coefficient is 0.472, and the graph density is 0.028 (see Figure 5.4). Although the treasurer lost the central position in the network, his node has the highest degree in the network – he is the person with the highest number of connections (80).

The macro network of the treasurer Ikhernefret reveals another important feature. Several individuals, two or two and a half generations ahead of his ego-network, are attested as bridges linking his 'world' to the networks

58 'The small world of the Abydos votive zone'

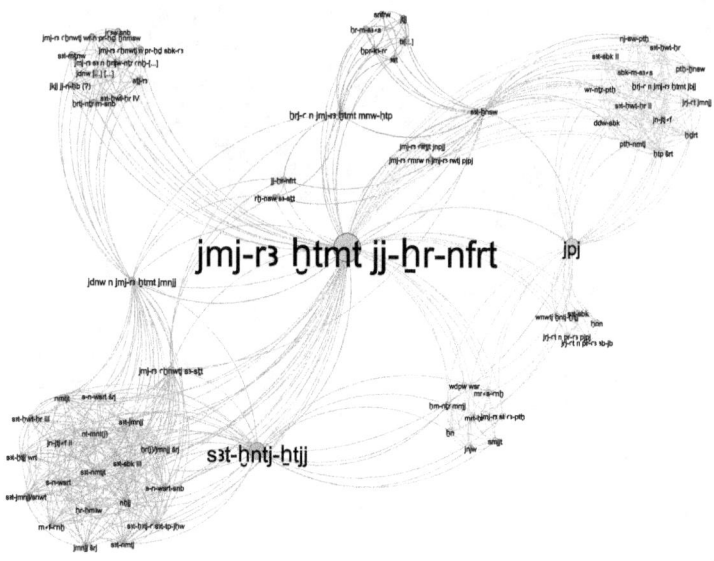

Figure 5.2 The ego-network of the treasurer Ikhernefret

of the two XIII Dynasty treasurers Senebsumai and Senebi,[49] respectively. Especially worth of mentioning is the 'bowman' (jrj-pḏt) nfr-n^3-jj[50] attested on the objects belonging to ANOC 44 (Firenze 2590, Louvre C 206 and München Gl. WAF 34) and linking the macro network of the treasurer Ikhernefret to the world of the treasurer Senebi.

5.3 The curious case of the lady rn(.j) n.j and ANOC XXII

The late XII Dynasty stela Cairo CG 20722 commemorates almost 50 individuals, most of whom are not related by kin ties. What brings them together on the object is their profession, as most of them are marked as 'sculptor' (qstj).[51] The holders of this title were responsible for work in stone including the carving of stelae, and were supervised by 'overseers' (mr) and/or 'section-overseers' (mr w'rt).

The stela CGC 20722 was assigned to the cluster ANOC XXII together with the stela CGC 20736.[52] Three dossiers linking the objects were identified: 'sculptor' (qstj) jbt,[53] 'sculptor' (qstj) d^{3}j-šwt.f,[54] and 'mistress of the house' (nbt pr) jk.[55]

The stela CGC 20722 records ten holders of the title qstj, five of whom are named jbt (further sculptors that are mentioned are jmnjj, 'nḫw, rn.f-snb,

'The small world of the Abydos votive zone' 59

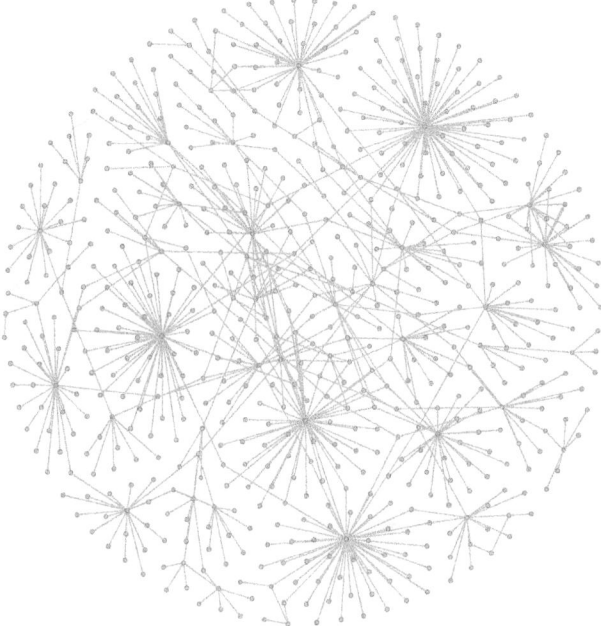

Figure 5.3 The two-mode macro network of Ikhernefret

sbk-ḥtp, and dꜣj-šwt.f). In some cases the text records just name and title, leaving open the possibility that the same person has been mentioned repeatedly in different registers; for other individuals mothers or spouses are named, which makes their distinction more feasible, but in most cases their relatives, if at all, are marked as 'his brother/his sister' (sn.f/snt.f), which may imply the wide range of family ties.[56]

A person with the same name and title, i.e., qstj jbt, was also mentioned on the stela Louvre C186. With several individuals not being clearly related to the sculptor jbt, the majority of the recorded persons belong to his family, including his father qstj nfrj, and his mother nbt-ḥwt. Following the name, title, and mother' name, Detlef Franke recognised that the same person is named on the offering table Cairo CG 23057.[57] The link between the two objects is further strengthened by the identification of the dossiers of the 'regulator of a watch' (mtj-n-sꜣ) nḫtj and his mother sꜣt-jn-ḥrt.[58]

Overall, six sculptors named jbt are known from approximately the same chronological framework. Would it be possible that the qstj jbt commemorated on the stela Louvre C 186 is one of the five sculptors with the same name recorded on CGC 20722? This is difficult to determine.

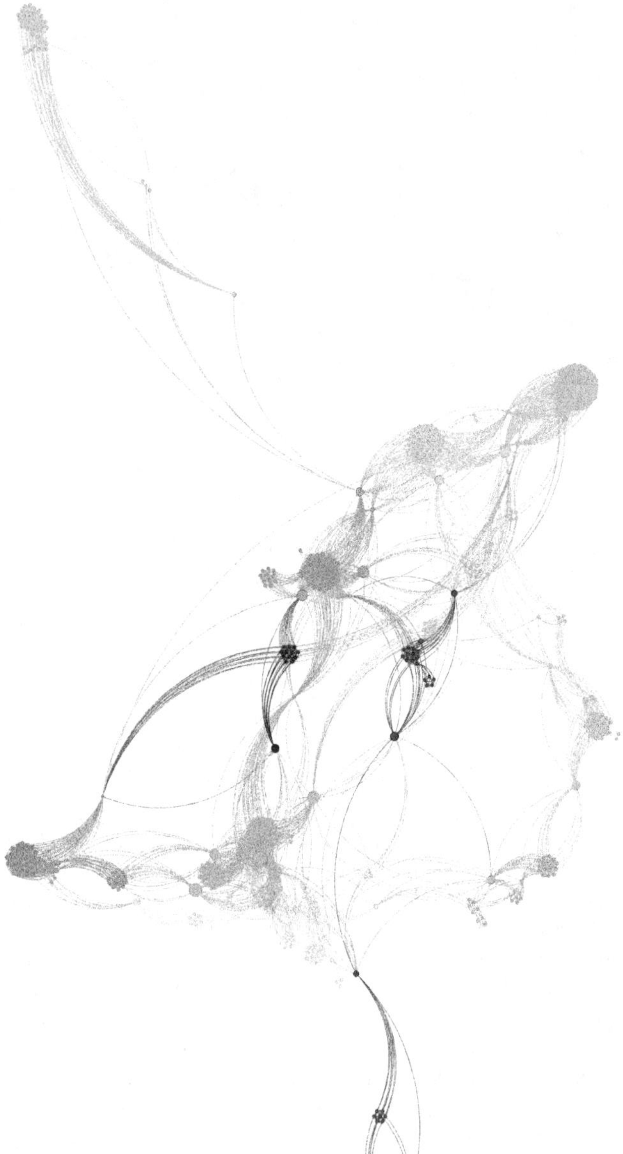

60 'The small world of the Abydos votive zone'

Figure 5.4 The one-mode macro network of Ikhernefret

'The small world of the Abydos votive zone' 61

However, the family tree of sculptor jbt attested on the stela Louvre C 186 (we may mark him as qstj jbt VI) provides the data, as already mentioned, of his mother (mwt.f) nbt-ḥwt, father (jt.f) qstj nfrj, and wife (ḥmt.f) sʲt-ḥwt-ḥr. Furthermore, the qstj nfrj is mentioned as the son of a lady mrjjt (i.e. jrj.n mrjjt). Three female figures that follow him (as represented on the stela) are marked as 'his sister': rn(.j)-n.j, jptt, and sʲt-tpjj, created of (jr(t.) n) sbbt. Based on the recorded data it seems that rn(.j)-n.j was the maternal sister of qstj nfrj, and the aunt of qstj jbt VI.

If we look back at the stela Cairo CGC 20722, commemorating qstj jbt, his wife sbbt, and six relatives (all marked as sn.f / snt.f), it should be noticed that a woman named rn(.j)-n.j, whose mother was mrjjt, is also attested on the object. The group of jbt's siblings is further identified by their mother named tnr. The same is true for the last figure in the register, namely mmj.

Knowing that *sn* ('brother') may indicate any male relative, it is tempting to consider that qstj jbt, a 'brother' of mrjjt on CGC 20722, is the same as the qstj jbt on Louvre C 186 (i.e., our qstj jbt VI). The identification is further strengthened by the fact that rn.j-n.j, born of mrjjt, is also marked as a sibling of qstj jbt on both objects.[59]

For most readers, it must be very tiresome to follow the text above and find the way out of the labyrinths of prosopography. The creation of genealogical charts is equally complicated, and reconstructing the hypothetical family tree described in the previous paragraphs is demanding and challenging. With the help of Social Network Analysis, the reconstructed network is presented in two-mode and one-mode graphs (see Figures 5.5 and 5.6).

Perhaps another hypothetical remark should be added. Stelae CG 20722 and CG 20736 are not only linked by prosopographic data; they are also produced in the same workshop.[60] Both of these aspects lead Abdel-Méguid El-Rabi'i to assign them to ANOC XXII. It is tempting to think that the stela Louvre C186 and the offering table CGC 23057 should be added either to the same, or to the envisaged adjacent chapel.

5.4 *Micro ego-networks as parts of the macro networks of treasurers Senbsumai and Senebi*

I have already addressed the network(s) of the treasurer Senebsumai, one of the best attested individuals of the XIII Dynasty, a contemporary of kings Khendjer through Neferhotep I.[61] However, several ego-networks of not so prominent individuals, existing rather on the periphery of his world, should be also acknowledged.

Prosopographic link(s) connecting the late Middle Kingdom stelae Cairo CG 20233, Rio de Janeiro 631, and Sinopoli Egi06 have been already noted.[62] This group of objects is chronologically determined by the stela Sinopoli Egi06, featuring the image of the treasurer Senebsumai.

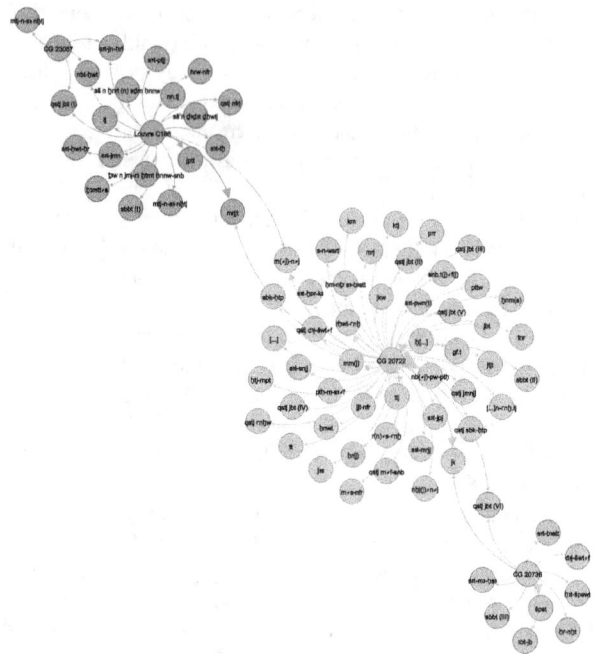

Figure 5.5 The two-mode network of the lady rn(.j)-n.j

Among the many individuals commemorated on the three stelae, the three (?) generations of women went almost unnoticed. The 'mistress of the house' (nbt pr) jw-bnrj (III), her offspring 'mistress of the house' (nbt pr) sȝt-jp, and her granddaughter 'mistress of the house' (nbt pr) n-jnj-st-jb belong to the branch of a family that was somehow related to the circle of the treasurer Senebsumai. The one-mode and two-mode networks of the given objects are presented in the following graphs (see Figures 5.7 and 5.8).

The stela Sinopoli Egi06 also features the 'great estate overseer' (mr pr wr) jmnjj.[63] He is a well attested individual recorded on several objects assigned to ANOC 10, to which stela Sinopoli Egi06 also belongs. The cluster of ANOC 10 will be discussed towards the end of the chapter.

Another elaborate network of mid- to high-ranking officials belonging to various administrative branches, their subordinates, and their families, chronologically bridging the time of treasurers Senebsumai and Senebi, has been recently exemplified, using the traditional prosopographic approach, by A. Ilin-Tomich.[64]

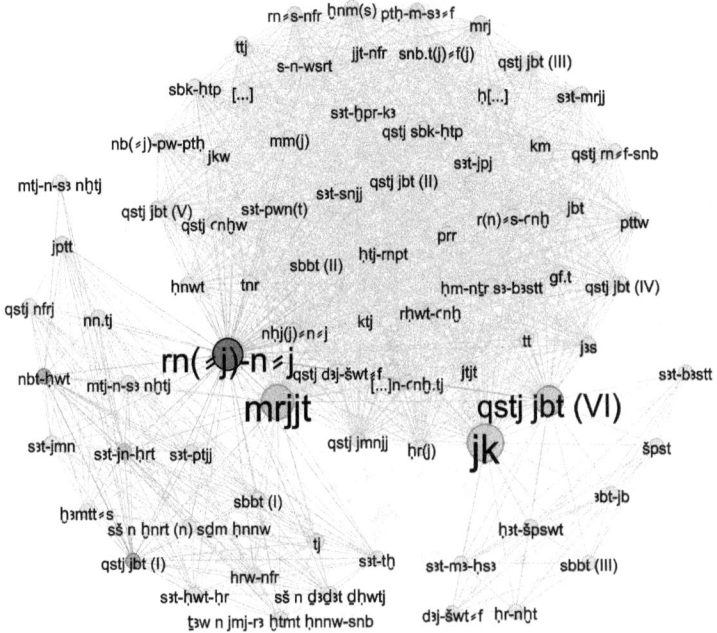

Figure 5.6 The one-mode network of the lady rn(.j)-n.j

Starting with the analysis of the data from the stela Durham EG582,[65] 11 additional objects were assigned to a prosopographic cluster. The identified dossiers and uniquely mentioned persons enabled the modelling of the network of 156 individuals and 1,671 edges, clustered into six groups (see Figures 5.9 and 5.10).

The modelled one-node graph (Figure 5.10) reveals several giant components, such as the one representing the 'interior overseer of the chamber of beer' (jmj-rȝ 'ḥnwtj n 't ḥnkwt) sn(.j)-pw.[66] Some of the objects featuring the 'interior overseer of the chamber of beer' sn(.j)-pw, as well as of other individuals from the pre Senebi network, are assigned to the ANOC 55.

The modelled 'pre Senebi network' can be linked to the elaborate and complex network of the treasurer Senebi, one of the best attested and most influential individuals who worked under Neferhotep I and Sobekhotep IV (c. 1747–1730 BC), rulers of the XIII Dynasty.[67]

Based on the preserved data Senebi appears on eight stelae predominantly attesting his colleagues and subordinates and thus providing a rich corpus of data for creating his social network(s).[68] As in the case of his predecessors

'The small world of the Abydos votive zone'

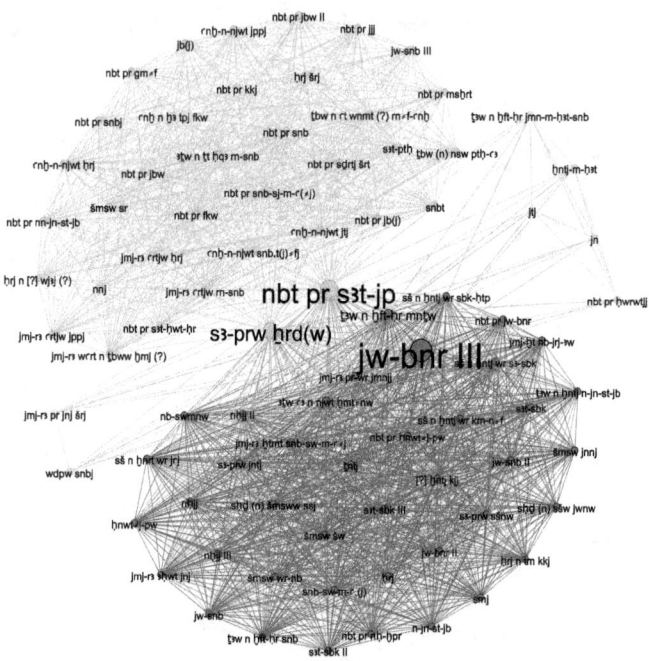

Figure 5.7 The one-mode network of the lady jw-bnrj (III)

Ikhernefret and Senebsumai, Senebi's family is the first collective or network he may belong to. However, his background was rather modest. The name of his father is usually abbreviated to nb(.j)-pw. He held the modest status marker of a 'man of the town' ('nḫ n njwt), just like the grandfather of Kings Neferhotep I and Sobekhotep IV, under whom Senebi served as treasurer. Senebi's mother was a 'mistress of the house' (nbt pr) named t-n(.j). Nothing is known about any wife or children.

The *cursus honorum* of Senebi is well known.[69] The first step in his career was, as far as we can trace it in sources, the office of the 'king's acquaintance' (rḫ-nswt), as stated on the stela Louvre C39. To be recognised as a 'king's acquaintance' meant to have a function in the court's hierarchy (the title could be used both as a ranking and regular title). In the same time this was an indication of both rank and status of an individual. Later in his career Senebi was promoted to the post of 'treasurer.' His career path may resemble a well-known late Middle Kingdom promotion pattern: from rḫ-nswt, through mr pr wr, to mr ḫtmt.[70]

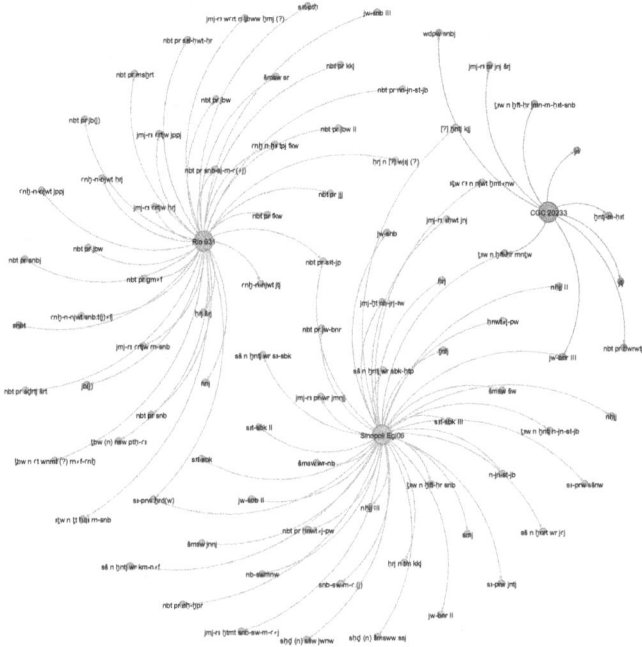

Figure 5.8 The two-mode network of the lady jw-bnrj (III)

People working in the administration of the 'treasurer' Senebi include several 'king's acquaintances.' For example, the stela Cairo GG 20614, commemorates Senebi, two 'interior-overseers of the Inner Palace' (mr ḫnwtj n k³p), and seven 'king's acquaintances.' The most prominent among them were Nebankh,[71] Senen,[72] and Rehuankh,[73] who are also well attested and have their own ego-networks.

It is also important to note that other prominent officials, who were 'royal sealers,' appeared together with Senebi on stelae. They were perhaps colleagues of the treasurer rather than his subordinates, although they were most likely ranked under him.

Another object from Senebi's corpus worth mentioning is the stela London BM EA 428.[74] The object displays several important individuals. Opposite Senebi, three officials stand in a row in a pose of reverence: a 'chief of tens of upper Egypt' (wr mḏw šmʿw), a 'bow keeper' (jrj-pḏt), and a 'scribe of the offering-table' (sš n wḏḥw) named Sauibptah. Based on the inscription Sauibptah enjoyed the status of ḫrd – a 'protégée' (literally 'child') of Senebi. This may be an indication of clientelistic network. As a 'scribe of

66   'The small world of the Abydos votive zone'

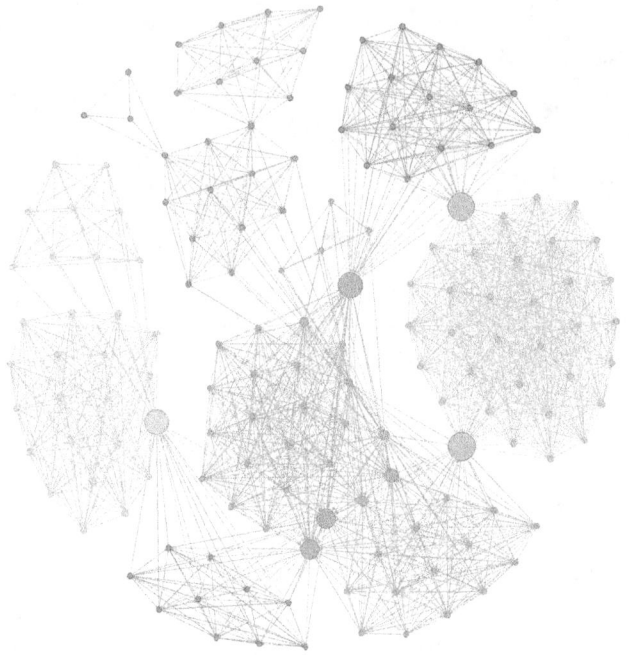

Figure 5.9 The one-mode network of the group of officials operating before the treasurer Senebi

the offering-table' working for a temple, he was responsible for registering the products to be offered to the gods, partly delivered by the royal treasury. Through this stela he honoured his highest superior (apart from the king), the treasurer, who was responsible for supplying the temple, and to whom he ultimately owed part of his income, but perhaps also his post (?). The 'chief of tens of upper Egypt' Nefersemen/Ptahadj was probably a 'link' between the treasury and the temple, although his exact relations to the other officials remain unexplained. However, it is tempting to consider that Senebi was also his patron.

The third register displays four individuals marked 'man of the town' ('nḫ n njwt). Perhaps they were part of the royal entourage (as conscripts or members of the household) or members of the local community of Abydos who participated in the festival honouring Osiris.

The lowest register presents medium-ranking officials of the central administration, who had perhaps been attached to Sauibptah during a royal commission at Abydos, supervised by Senebi or by the 'chief of tens of upper

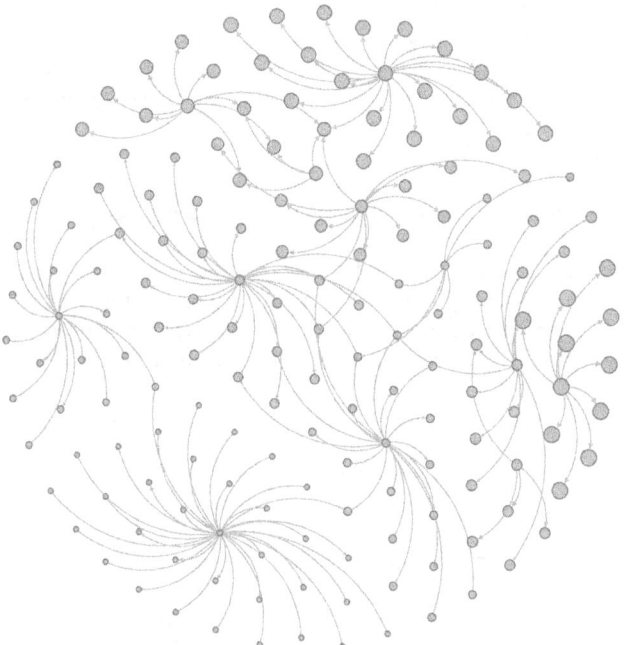

Figure 5.10 The two-mode network of the group of officials operating before the treasurer Senebi

Egypt' Nefersemen/Ptah-adj. The theophorous names Sauibptah and Ptah-adj strongly suggest a Memphite origin to at least these two officials. Probably the whole group was sent out to Abydos from the capital at Lisht.

The stela Liverpool M13635, destroyed in the Second World War, is also worth mentioning. The inscription records the name of Senebi's father, 'two chamberlains,' and 'overseers of Lower Egypt' (mr ꜥḫnwtj; mr tꜣ-mḥw), but also the 'king's son' (sꜣ-nswt) ḥdr, whose mother was the 'king's daughter' (sꜣt-nswt) sꜣt-ḫntj-ḫtjj. Both individuals refer to the family of the XIII Dynasty king Khendjer, and can be considered as a link to the global court network of the Late Middle Kingdom.

Senebi is also attested, along with the already mentioned 'king's acquaintance' Nebankh, in a rock inscription on Sehel Island mentioning the family of king Neferhotep I, which again brings him to the court network.

Nothing is known about the chapel of Senebi at Abydos. Furthermore, not a single monument is known to have been dedicated by him at Abydos. All the Abydene stelae that feature the treasurer Senebi came either from the cemeteries beside the processional road and temple area, or from memorial chapels (ANOC).

However, his close associate, the 'king's acquaintance' Rehuankh, very probably had a chapel of his own at Abydos – ANOC 22, which will be discussed later – including three stelae. One of these objects, namely the stela Vienna ÄS 140, displays the treasurer Senebi.

It is unknown how long Senebi held the office. His contemporaries, Nebankh and Rehuankh, still worked for Neferhotep's brother, King Sobekhotep IV, who likewise ordered construction works in the Osiris temple complex.

The relational data recorded on stelae mentioning the treasurer Senebi are important for reconstructing careers, hierarchies, and social structures, i.e., for sociography and detecting network ties. The treasurer's elaborated network (see Figure 5.11), although still incomplete, consists of 1,070 nodes, 25

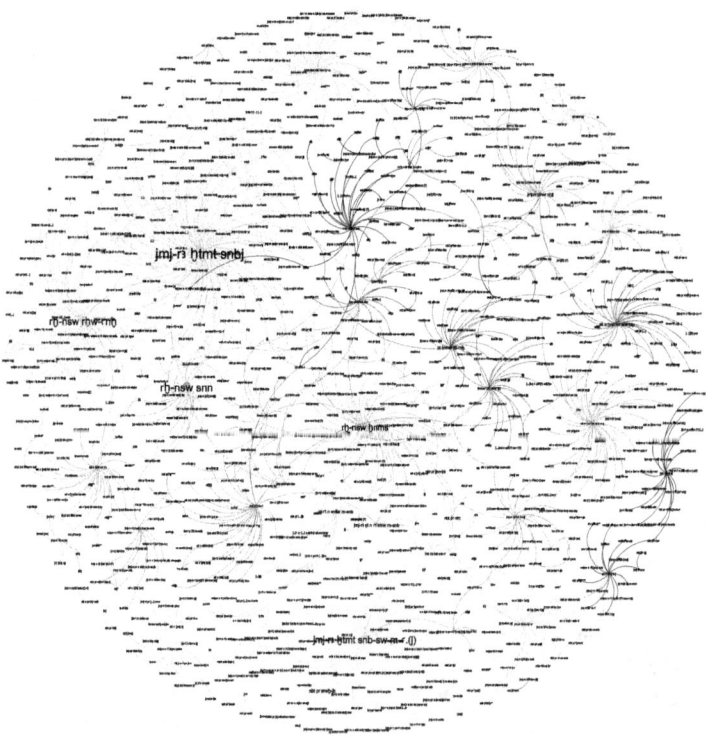

Figure 5.11 Simplified one-mode network of the treasurer Senebi

clusters and 1,213 filtered edges. With 120 direct links, Senebi is the key-figure of the network (his betweenness centrality is 0.183). The maximum path length of Senebi's network is 6, and the average path length is 1.99, while the average clustering coefficient is 0.060. As expected, following Senebi in degree centrality (number of ties) are his predecessors Senebsumai (71), Rehuankh (62), and Nebankh (49).

There is another important aspect, revealed by the modelled network of the treasurer Senebi, which needs to be mentioned. The social structure of the individuals, marked by their titles and status markers, belonging to the circle of Senebi, the important successor of Senebsumai, differs from that of Senebsumai. While several stelae feature members of Senebsumai's private household, mainly his 'store overseers' (mr st),[75] no such people appear on stelae for Senebi, which predominantly feature his subordinates and protégés. Perhaps something has changed in the custom of commemorating treasurers over the period when Senebsumai and Senebi held that position, and this change is also reflected in the graphs exemplifying their records.

5.5 The 'small world' of the Abydos votive zone – the game of graphs, glyphs, and objects

The individual monuments, most of them being stelae, in the cultic landscape of Abydos have been interpreted, as already mentioned, as memorial chapels that aim to perpetuate the participation of an individual, or a group of people, in the celebration of the festivals of Osiris for eternity. William Kelly Simpson's initial idea when organising material into ANOC (Abydos North Offering Chapel) groups was that chapels may point towards the existence, in addition to the obvious architectural gatherings, of some sort of grouping of people belonging to various social strata, since the small memorial chapels could perhaps belong to relatives, colleagues, or dependants of the owner of the larger ones.[76] Starting with this idea, the recognition and reconstruction of ANOC groups would eventually lead to the mapping of the ritual and social landscape of Abydos.

Certainly, prosopography is not the only research field that benefits from ANOC clusters. The material assigned to chapels has also been analysed from the perspective of the workshop, i.e., based on the creation of 'artistic and/ or production dossiers.' The workshop consists, as Freed stated, of "three or more stelae sharing distinctive aspects of composition or style which collectively set them apart from others."[77] However, as Olabarria rightly pointed out, and this is obvious to anyone working with Abydos material, the idea that stelae workshops are a material expression of family groups should be avoided:

> Despite some commonalities derived from the nature of the objects of study, kin groups, ANOC groups and workshops are essentially different

in the type of analytical category they intend to reconstruct. A feature that brings kin groups, ANOC groups and workshops together is that they are all etic terms, i.e. classifications devised by researchers that may or may not have been significant to ancient Egyptians.[78]

As can be observed from the examples discussed above, data for the reconstruction of individual dossiers, kin groups, and network datasets initially created from the objects assigned to ANOC chapels often need to be complemented with sources originating from other sites.[79]

Another important aspect for analysing material from the votive zone, is that the spatial and diachronic aspects of ANOC clusters should be approached and understood within the ritual landscape of Abydos, where individuals, kin groups, high-ranking and low-ranking officials sought for eternal participation in the festivities of Osiris. As exemplified by J. Kopleff, based on her survey of ANOC 29 and ANOC 52, although there are significant differences between the analysed clusters (in chronology, ranks and titles of the recorded individuals, and quality of object production), they share basic common features.[80] ANOC 29, commemorating 'estate overseer' (mr pr) Hor (early XII Dynasty),[81] and ANOC 52, of the 'reporter of the vizier' (wḥmw n ṯitj) Senwosret (early XIII Dynasty),[82] equally reveal one and the same expectation on the part of the dedicants: a desire to benefit from the rituals in the votive zone and from closeness to the deity himself.

Leire Olabarria made another important step towards the understanding of the Abydos votive zone and ANOC clusters with the introduction of the concept of koinography, which focuses on tracing the group (koinê) "based on the idea that social groups, and not individuals, should be treated as the preferred unit of social analysis, and that the factor of time is a fundamental tool to explore the position and role of that group in wider society."[83] Olabarria also rightly argues that the distinction between kin groups as a social unit and clusters of monuments should not be overlooked, since more than one kin group may be present on one stela.

Olabarria's book centres on three 'koinographic' case studies. She chooses ANOC 12 as a starting point and an example of the birth of a kin group, ANOC 28 as a case study of a kin group at its peak, and ANOC VI focusing on a kin group in decline. The 'koinographic' approach, rather new in Egyptology, more fully considers the social groupings represented on the stelae.[84]

Equally important to keep in mind when analysing ANOC chapels are rules of decorum and display, since clusters are governed by both of them. Overall, for Olabarria:

> The intricacies of their portrayal of the social structure can only be decoded if the monumental record and the ways it relates to lived experience are understood in emic terms.[85]

Indeed, each ANOC cluster, regardless of size, type, or number of attached objects, as well as of chronological context, is distinctive in its own way – in materiality, style, and commemorated individuals. It is also obvious that ANOC chapels share common features: titles, chronological frameworks, workshop attributions, stylistic contents, and the deep and strong wishes of people to be in the presence of the god Osiris.

Is the symbolic presence of a person in one chapel sufficient? Imagine being in the presence of the god not just in one, but in several chapels. Or alternatively, on more than one object. Perhaps even in more than one ANOC?

One aspect of ANOC clusters that has escaped researchers' attention is the possibility of 'linking' various clusters through individuals commemorated on objects assigned to them. In prosopographic studies, we detect the dossiers of individuals looking for attestations on individual objects. However, would it be possible to look for individuals attested in various ANOC chapels? If so, would it be feasible to link, or in other words to model, a network of ANOC clusters though the individuals bridging them? The answer is positive for both questions.

The first linked group of chapels which I was able to identify include three clusters: ANOCs 7, 19, and 32.

ANOC 7 is an assemblage of three objects from the early XIII Dynasty: stelae Cairo CG 20768, Leiden Inv. L.XI.21, and offering table Cairo CG 23210.[86] The most prominent individual on the objects of ANOC 7 is rdj-n.j-ptḥ,[87] who held the title of 'overseer of the troop of stonemasons' (mr mšʿ n ḥrtjw-nṯr).[88] The most elaborated object of the group is the stela Leiden L.XI.2, commemorating rdj-n.j-ptḥ's family and some of his subordinate colleagues (i.e., stonemasons). The pedestal London BM EA 177, although not listed to the ANOC, obviously belongs to the same group.[89]

ANOC 19, dating to the first half of XIII Dynasty, is a cluster of eight objects: stelae Cairo CG 20087 and 20100, Manchester 2963, Bolton 10.20/11, Cairo JE 39069, London BM EA 210, Garstang E.31, and Garstang 321d. The complex structure of ANOC 19, which in reality most probably consisted of more than one chapel, features four prominent individuals and their families and colleagues.[90] They are: 'high steward' (mr pr wr)[91] jmn-m-ḥ3t-snb/nmtj-m-wsḫt,[92] 'the scribal assistant (bearer) of (documents concerning) earth (work)' (ṯ3w n s3tw)[93] jjj,[94] 'deputy treasurer' (jdnw n mrḫtmt)[95] nṯrw-r-ʿw,[96] and the 'overseer of sealers' (ḫtmw-bjtj; mr ḫtmtjw)[97] ʿkj.[98] The high steward jmn-m-ḥ3t-snb/nmtj-m-wsḫt, as recorded on the stela Cairo CG 20100, was the owner of a špsj chapel in Abydos. What brought all these people together, being of different social status, is not clear, although there is a possibility that they belonged to the administration of the town of Wah-Sut.[99]

The objects assigned to ANOC 32 are stelae Cairo CG 20520, Florence 2561, and Florence 2559.[100] All of them feature the 'chief of tens of Upper Egypt' (wr mḏw šmʿw)[101] nḫjj,[102] his father the 'overseer of marshland-dwellers' (mr sḫtjw)[103] ḫʿ-ḫpr-rʿ-snb,[104] and their colleagues and family members.

Although the individual ANOC clusters were physically defined and apparently isolated within the cultic landscape of the Votive zone, a closer look at the prosopographic data reveals that some persons are attested on the objects belonging to different memorial chapels. The same is true for ANOCs 7, 19, and 32, which are linked through several individuals.

Person who are bridges between clusters are: the 'count and overseer of the temple precinct' (ḥ3tj-'; mrḥwt-nṯr[105]) rn-snb (Cairo CG 20087 = ANOC 19 and Cairo CG 20520 = ANOC 32),[106] 'estate overseer' (mr pr) nmtj-wr (Leiden L.XI.2 = ANOC 7 and CG 20520 = ANOC 32),[107] 'mistress of the house' (nb pr) psḏt,[108] and 'mistress of the house' (nbt pr) nj.t-ḥd (Leiden L.XI.2 = ANOC 7 and CG 20520 = ANOC 32).

The dossiers of the individuals bridging the analysed ANOC clusters are not very revealing. The 'estate overseer' (mr pr) nmtj-wr, attested on the stelae Leiden L.XI.2 (ANOC 7) and CG 20520 (ANOC 32), cannot be clearly linked with the main persons on any of the objects. The female links are weak, relying just on the names and title, which are most common. However, it is worth mentioning that apart from the monuments of ANOC 7, 'overseers of stonemason crews' (mr ḥrtjw-nṯr) occur on the stelae Cairo CG 20100 (snb – ANOC 19) and Cairo CG 20520 (snb.f-šrj – ANOC 32).

To highlight the ties between the individuals attested on the chosen ANOC clusters, and between the ANOCs themselves, the network approach has been applied to the data originating from the assigned objects by generating one and two-mode networks.

The starting points of any network are actors, or entities (i.e., nodes), and the connections (i.e., edges) between them. A network based on prosopographic data is an assemblage of individual actors and their mutual relations. More precisely, and not restricted to prosopographic data, the network manifests relational links between individuals and/or objects within the physical, social, and temporal contexts. The generated network data were analysed by focusing on the relational patterns of network elements through the application of graph theory.[109]

As previously mentioned, defining nodes is the starting point for any network. The nodes can belong to the same type of entity (humans), creating (or resulting in) a one-mode network, or to two different types (for example, individuals and ANOC clusters, or objects on which they appear), resulting in a two-mode or bipartite network. Although many Social Network Analysis tools have been developed to investigate the relationships between individuals or between groups of individuals, they can be also applied on different types of entities that do not directly pertain to social relations, or are not human.[110]

The modelled monopartite network (where *nodes* are persons attested on objects, and *edges* are connections among them) represents a visualisation of the ego-networks, or clusters, of the individuals featuring on the objects assigned to ANOCs 7, 19, and 32.

The modelled one-mode graph revealed 140 individuals and 3,675 edges. The ego-networks of prominent, or perhaps better to say well attested, individuals featuring on the given objects provide insight into familial, collegial, and/or institutional and clientelistic patterns. Furthermore, the reconstructed network (with a great caution regarding its partiality) may imply a 'small world' model of prominent individuals,[111] with a number of separate network clusters, each comprising nodes connected to each other by 'strong ties' (a sociological term referring to a close relationship, e.g., of family, friends, or colleagues) which are joined together by a few 'weak ties.'[112] These 'weak ties' are bridges between distant groups within the network.

The 'network approaches,' and the idea that ANOC clusters can be perhaps regarded as elements, or actants, of an envisaged 'community,' lead to the possible existence of the 'small world' of the Abydos votive zone. As already mentioned, in basic formal terms, a network is comprised of nodes and ties: nodes are entities or agents, and ties are the links between these entities.[113] Thus, there are two elements, and the network is comprised of the 'relationships' between them. These relationships can be assessed as structures that they generate in the network more broadly.

For detecting an ego-network of individuals attested on the objects belonging to ANOC clusters, Social Network Analysis is the most suitable approach. However, for mapping and modelling the network(s) of the ANOC memorial chapels, Actor-Network Theory (ANT) would be more comprehensible. Actor-Network Theory incorporates the symmetry of agency between human and non-human participants, based on the premise that inanimate objects (in our case ANOC chapels) actively participate in shaping society.[114] In this case, the network is concerned with the interactions and entanglements between humans (attested on objects assigned to ANOC groups), the ANOC chapels, and the landscape of the Abydos votive zone.[115] In ANT theory, all participants in the 'process,' both human and non-human, are actors or actants with the capacity to act and behave and reshape the world.[116] According to Actor-Network Theory, material and human actants may manifest themselves in the same network, each having agency and each being co-dependent on each other. To simplify things, human and non-human nodes interact with each other in a relational web or modelled network.

Thus, we may introduce the ANOC as a hypothetical type of node and try to see how they are linked together. The modelled two-mode network of ANOC clusters 7, 19 and 32 relaying on the same assemblage of data as the one-mode graph (see Figure 5.13), clearly visualised the bridges - 'weak ties' (individuals attested in more than one cluster)[117] – linking the 'small worlds' of memorial chapels.

The one- and two-mode networks created from the data of ANOCs 7, 19, and 32 represent sample network models for identifying patterns of supposedly 'social' relations among individuals and objects.

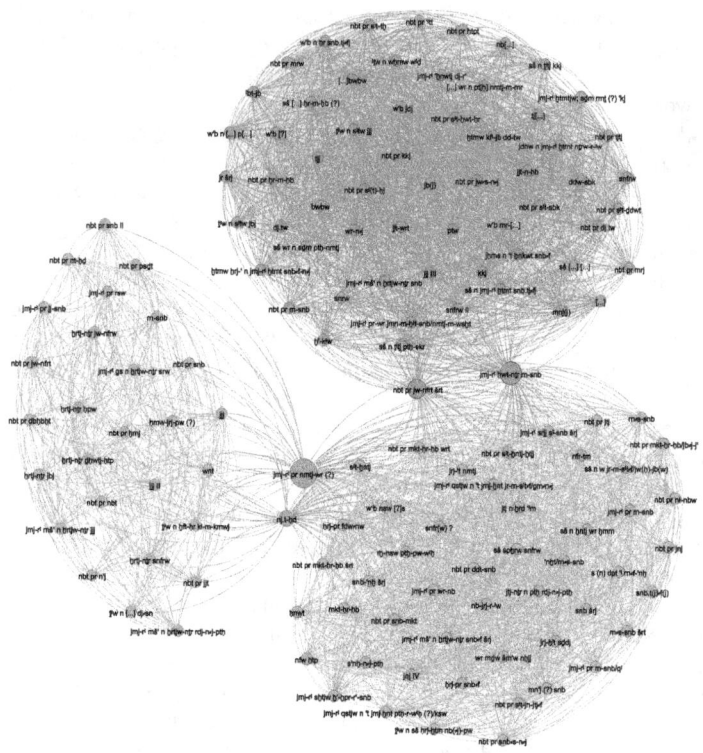

Figure 5.12 One-mode network of the ANOC 7, 19 and 32

The recognised relatedness and modelled networks of ANOCs 7, 19, and 32 are not an exception. Two more groups of connected clusters were also identified: one incorporating ANOCs 16, 52, and 57, and the other linking ANOCs 17, 22, 25, and V. It is important to mention that the largest group of ANOC chapels also belongs to the macro network of the treasurer Senebi. However, the three recognised groups are not isolated – although the ties are weak, all of them are mutually linked. Ten ANOCs, encompassing 42 objects and 363 individuals, were connected through individuals (bridging them) ranging from one to five (see Figures 5.14 and 5.15).

Although it is known that the given clusters are from the Late Middle Kingdom, the recognised connectivity would ask for a closer look at their chronological frameworks and the generations of individuals attested on them. Almost 30 years ago Charles Wetherell and Barry Wellman[118] argued that network studies offered important new ways of conceptualising communities.

'The small world of the Abydos votive zone' 75

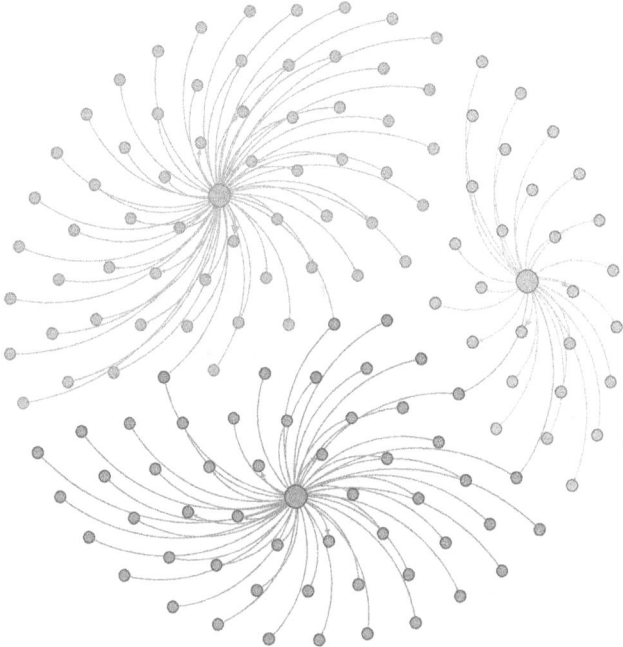

Figure 5.13 Two-mode network of ANOCs 7, 19, and 32

Looking for further cross-connections through network theory, the Abydos votive zone network can be expanded and better contextualised.

What is the purpose and relevance of all the graphs? What are they supposed to represent? What is the relevance of a created network bearing in mind that we do not know either how many clusters existed within the votive zone, nor to what degree the objects assigned to the identified ANOCs reflect their completeness?

The word 'game' appears in the title of this chapter and in the name of its final subchapter. In both cases the word 'game' is used as a metaphor – any game implies rules, but with an uncertain outcome. This is exactly what we are doing when implementing SNA – we are feeding software with data (either from written sources – glyphs, i.e., hieroglyphs – or objects – i.e., archaeological data), applying strict rules (various metrics and algorithms), and achieving a result with all uncertainties – the graph, or sociogram.

Thinking in terms of the links between entities (either individuals or chapels) and the way these relationships structure the broader network, rather than thinking solely about the entities, is methodologically exciting. The micro-network of the lady jw-bnrj, or the macro-network of the treasurer Senebi,

Figure 5.14 The one-mode network of the ten ANOC clusters with 363 individuals and 9,372 links

strongly reflects the complexity of the society and social structure of the Late Middle Kingdom. Relying on the nature of the analysed entities from a network perspective, the focus shifts from the attributes of the data towards the relations between them, and the position of the data in the network. The detected relationships (or links) can be analysed in a number of ways: through interactions that are located spatially, those that are social, relational, or institutional; or through a consideration of the different types of entities within the same network (for example, people and objects produced in 'x place,' people and places originating from it).[119] Second, the created network(s) may provide hints for filling the gaps within the chronological frameworks of the careers of certain individuals, or to provide a more stable dating (either to confirm or challenge the established one) for certain objects or ANOCs. Third, despite the assertion of Anna Collar that there must be awareness "that a representation of

'The small world of the Abydos votive zone' 77

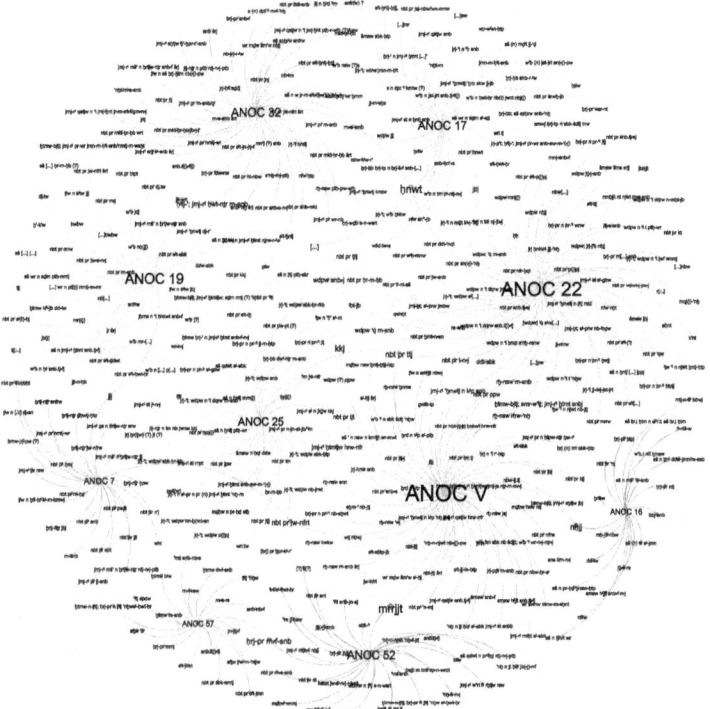

Figure 5.15 The two-mode network of the ten ANOC clusters

a network drawn from selected data does not necessarily represent a past network,"[120] network analysis is also valid with incomplete datasets.[121] The same is true for any source of information, either written or archaeological, that we are dealing with from the distant past. Any single discovery may profoundly change our knowledge of an event, or the period that we are interested about. As the material from Göbekli Tepe profoundly changed our understanding of the Preceramic Neolithic, new data from Abydos may shift our perception of the votive zone. For the time being, we must rely on available datasets.

Finally, through the tools of Social Network Analysis and the particularities of the given relational datasets, it is possible to outline the hypothetical model(s) in which the structure of the surviving ANOC datasets reflect (perhaps!) the original distribution of assigned objects and individuals. If we set aside visualisation (which may or may not be important), a new approach towards a more comprehensive understanding of social relations, prosopography, interconnections, and even chronology (especially regarding generation

'The small world of the Abydos votive zone'

sequences) may be envisaged. In reaching this goal, Social Network Analysis and Actor-Network Theory may be our greatest support.

Notes

1 A comprehensible, brief summary of the history of excavations at Abydos can be found on the website of the project Artefacts of Excavation. British Excavations in Egypt 1880–1980. See https://egyptartefacts.griffith.ox.ac.uk/site/abydos (accessed August 29, 2023). Depending on the period, and/or the special attention of the research team, it would be difficult to provide a relevant list of publications without omitting some important contributions. For a general overview, with references for further reading, see Wegner (1996); O'Connor (2009); Effland and Effland (2013); Regulski (2019); Budka (2019); Cahail (2022).
2 Wegner (2001); Olabarria (2020a), 28–40; Wegner et al. (2021); Cahail (2022).
3 Effland et al. (2010).
4 Wegner (2009), 143–149.
5 Leahy (1989), 56–57; Effland et al. (2010).
6 Smith (2017).
7 The Osiris procession is the best-known aspect of the ritual performed in Abydos (Kucharek, 2006). The earliest textual references mentioning aspects of the Osiris procession in Abydos came from two stelae of the early XI Dynasty. See Oppenheim et al. (2015), 42–43 and Wegner et al. (2021), 148–157.
8 See Volokhine (1998).
9 In Ancient Egypt, stelae were inscribed or painted slabs of stone or wood, rarely of metal, or were cut directly into rock, containing inscriptions and/or images, commissioned by a person (royal or non-royal) as a means of commemoration or praise. They were set up in a special place (commemorating an event, or a visit to a special location, a royal commission, etc.), in a temple, in offering chapels, or in a tomb. Stelae were often produced in a workshop and could range widely in quality, size, and style (which, again, may depend greatly on the person who commissioned them, but also on the style of the workshop and artisans involved in their production). Some were large and finely carved with exacting attention to interior detailing. For stelae in Abydos see most recently Snape (2019) and Olabarria (2020a).
10 Simpson (1974), 11–13; Lichtheim (1988), 131; Yamamoto (2015). This area is also referred to as the 'Abydos North Offering Chapel (ANOC) zone,' the 'votive zone,' the 'North Cemetery,' the 'Portal Temple area,' the 'cenotaph zone,' 'Abydos North' and 'North Abydos.'
11 See O'Connor (1985); Leprohon (2019); Olabarria (2020a); Olabarria (2020b). Many of the preserved texts request that the stelae act as proxies for chapel owners, so that they can forever participate in the cult of Osiris-Khentiamentiu and the annual festival of the god held there. Their wishes are sometimes elaborated with

the so-called Abydos Formula, a list of requests for the afterlife. See Lichtheim (1988), 55–58, 114–116.
12 Snape (2019); Adams (2010); Olabarria (2020a), 48–62.
13 However, any discussion of stelae, their dedicants and persons recorded on them need to consider another important aspect – who commissioned them, for whom, and why. Although many objects, including stelae, were commissioned by the people mentioned on them, the concept of patronage must also be considered. Patronage, of either the royal or elite variety, is an issue that may also have affected the size, quality, workshop, and place of production for the stelae belonging to officials. See Moreno García (2013) and (2020).
14 Landgráfová (2011), no. 41.
15 Oppenheim (2015), 25.
16 Wegner (2015), 318.
17 Snape (2011), 125.
18 Simpson (1974).
19 O'Connor (1985) and his team identified two main types of memorial chapel. Building on previous work, Yamamoto (2009, 35–45) described six.
20 Simpson (1974), 1–16.
21 Cooney (1974); Spaull (1975); Berlev (1976); De Meulenaere (1977); El-Rabi'i (1977); Andreu (1980); Silverman (1977); DeVries (1977); Franke (1984); Berlev (1987); Roccati (2003); Grajetzki and Stefanović (2012); Olabarria (2020a). See also Ilin-Tomich (2017), 137, table 47.
22 El-Rabi'i (1977).
23 Olabarria (2020a), 205–222.
24 See Simpson (1974), 1–2, 6, 8–9; O'Connor (2009), 26–27; Kopleff (2017), 13–14.
25 Simpson (1974), 11; Snape (2019), 255–256; Olabarria (2020a), 35–41; Olabarria (2020b); Pillon (2022), 454–467.
26 Simpson (1974), 10–11.
27 Simpson (1974), 12.
28 O'Connor (1985), 164, 166; Végh (2019), 301–303; Olabarria (2020b). The inscription on Cairo CG 20733 reads: jr.n(.j) grt t³ mꜥḥꜥt m ꜣbḏw m ḏbt sḥt.n.j – "(I) built this mꜥḥꜥt in Abydos of bricks that I moulded myself."
29 Herzberg (2019), 40; Herzberg-Beiersdorf (2023), 369–401.
30 For the definition of the social capital as "resources that are based on membership in a group" see Bourdieu (1983), 191.
31 See for example (Rosell) 2021.
32 Olabarria (2020a) 61; see also Landvatter (2021).
33 Simpson (1974), 4.
34 Simpson (1974), 4; O'Connor (1985). The plan of the memorial chapel area at Abydos shows how smaller chapels were built adjacent to larger ones; see O'Connor (1985), 168.
35 Revez (2003); see also Moreno García (2013); Olabarria (2020a), 126–127.
36 See Chollier (2019).
37 Olabarria (2020a), 41.
38 Ilin-Tomich (2017, 80–82) identified that stelae belonging to the ANOC 1 group were produced in two different workshops: Memphis-Faiyum Region Workshop 1 and Memphis-Faiyum Region Workshop 2. See also Olabarria (2014), 129–131.
39 Franke (1984), 1, 27, 94, 155, 235, 254, 543, 551, 705, 770, 779; Grajetzki and Stefanović (2012), 234.
40 Franke (1984), 27; Grajetzki (2000), 56–57 and (2009), 57–59. Stefanović (2019a), 270–274. See also *Persons and Names of the Middle Kingdom*, Version 4 (person 27; accessed August 2, 2023), https://pnm.uni-mainz.de/person/27.

41 Franke (1984), 551; See also *Persons and Names of the Middle Kingdom*, Version 4 (person 27; accessed August 2, 2023), https://pnm.uni-mainz.de/person/551.
42 The title 'treasurer' is attested within the branches of the central administration, as well as in the provinces. Those who worked at the court were identified by additional ranking titles. Treasurers were greatly involved in sealing goods, as exemplified by the high number of attestations of the office itself on scarabs and scarab seals. See Grajetzki (2000), 43–78, 2009, 16–18, 44–46, 67–100; Grajetzki (2013), 238–247; Quirke (2004), 48–84 and 85–96; Quirke (1990), 58–61. See also *Persons and Names of the Middle Kingdom*, Version 4 (title 1; accessed August 2, 2023), https://pnm.uni-mainz.de/title/1.
43 Lichtheim (1988), 98–100.
44 Simpson et al. (2003), 426–427.
45 Social Network Analysis (SNA) is a sociological, graph theory–based approach used to investigate social structures created by the patterns of relationships (ties or links) between actors (nodes). For an introduction to SNA see Barabási (2003); Wasserman and Faust (1994); Newman (2010); Scott and Carrington (2011); Brughmans (2013); Brughmans and Peeples (2017); Mills (2017); Pálsson (2020); Brughmans and Peeples (2023). The most important terms specific to SNA jargon are based on the glossary of Brughmans and Peeples (2023).
46 Stefanović (2016), 318.
47 As a rule, the networks modelled from the datasets created from ancient sources have taken this two-step approach: a) creating a two-mode network, and b) collapsing it into a one-mode graph in which nodes of one type are treated as the edges that link the nodes of the other type. By means of collapsing (parts of) the two-mode network(s) in this manner and comparing results with the one-mode model(s) reflecting the *content* of the studied documents, strengths and shortcomings of either method could also be identified and discussed.
48 Stefanović (2019a), 270–274.
49 Stefanovic (2019a) and (2020).
50 Franke (1984), 309; see also *Persons and Names of the Middle Kingdom*, Version 4 (person 309; accessed August 2, 2023) https://pnm.uni-mainz.de/person/309.
51 Ward (1982), 1561; see also *Persons and Names of the Middle Kingdom*, Version 4 (title 99; accessed August 2, 2023) https://pnm.uni-mainz.de/title/99.
52 El-Rabi'i (1977), 21.
53 Franke (1984), 67; see also *Persons and Names of the Middle Kingdom*, Version 4 (person 67; accessed August 2, 2023) https://pnm.uni-mainz.de/person/67.
54 Franke (1984), 739; see also *Persons and Names of the Middle Kingdom*, Version 4 (person 739; accessed August 2, 2023) https://pnm.uni-mainz.de/person/739.
55 *Persons and Names of the Middle Kingdom*, Version 4 (person 2039; accessed August 2, 2023) https://pnm.uni-mainz.de/person/2039.
56 For the stela CG 20722 see Franke (1983), 91.
57 Franke (1984), 66; Stefanović (2016), 138 (for his mother nbt-ḥwt). See also *Persons and Names of the Middle Kingdom*, Version 4 (person 66; accessed August 2, 2023) https://pnm.uni-mainz.de/person/66.
58 Franke (1984) and Stefanović (2016), 248. See also *Persons and Names of the Middle Kingdom*, Version 4 (person 348; accessed August 2, 2023) https://pnm.uni-mainz.de/person/348.
59 Consequently, stela CGC 20722 should be added to the Franke (1984), 66. The dossier of rn.j-n.j should be also acknowledged.
60 Ilin-Tomich (2017), 215.
61 Stefanović (2019a), 275–278. See also Franke (1984), 666 and 667; Grajetzki (2000), 57–59; Grajetzki (2001), 12–25; Franke and Marée (2013), 50; see also

Persons and Names of the Middle Kingdom, Version 4 (person 668; accessed August 2, 2023) https://pnm.uni-mainz.de/person/668.
62 Ilin-Tomich (2014), 143 (14); Stefanović (2019b), 181.
63 Franke (1984), 98; see also *Persons and Names of the Middle Kingdom*, Version 4 (person 98; accessed August 2, 2023) https://pnm.uni-mainz.de/person/98.
64 Ilin-Tomich (2023).
65 *Persons and Names of the Middle Kingdom*, Version 4 (inscription 5739; accessed August 2, 2023) https://pnm.uni-mainz.de/inscription/5739.
66 See Franke (1984), 599; *Persons and Names of the Middle Kingdom*, Version 4 (person 599; accessed August 2, 2023) https://pnm.uni-mainz.de/person/599.
67 Franke (1984), *Persons and Names of the Middle Kingdom*, Version 4 (person 634; accessed August 2, 2023) https://pnm.uni-mainz.de/person/634. See Grajetzki 2000, 56–57, 2001; Franke and Marée (2013), 156–158.
68 See Franke (1984), 70, 96, 97, 115, 120, 294; 300, 559, 599, 600, 606, 693; Grajetzki and Stefanović (2012), 102; Stefanović (2020).
69 Grajetzki (2001), and (2009).
70 Grajetzki (2001); Franke and Marée (2013), 49.
71 Franke (1984), 294; *Persons and Names of the Middle Kingdom*, Version 4 (person 294; accessed August 2, 2023) https://pnm.uni-mainz.de/person/294.
72 Franke (1984), 682; *Persons and Names of the Middle Kingdom*, Version 4 (person 682; accessed August 2, 2023) https://pnm.uni-mainz.de/person/682.
73 Franke (1984), 389; *Persons and Names of the Middle Kingdom*, Version 4 (person 389; accessed August 2, 2023) https://pnm.uni-mainz.de/person/389.
74 Franke and Marée (2013), 153–158.
75 Quirke (2004), 66.
76 Simpson (1974), 4; O'Connor (1985). See also Wegner (2001), 10 and, for a more anthropological perspective, Olabarria (2020a), 60–63 and (2020b).
77 Freed (1996), 298. See Marée (2010); Ilin-Tomich (2017). See also Olabarria (2020a), 60–63 and (2020b) for limitations and obstacles of approaching stelae and other monumental sources from the point of view of their materiality.
78 Olabarria (2020a), 62.
79 Which advocates against the initial idea of W. K. Simpson (1974, 13) about the reconstruction of families.
80 Kopleff (2017).
81 Franke (1984), 424; *Persons and Names of the Middle Kingdom*, Version 4 (person 424; accessed August 2, 2023) https://pnm.uni-mainz.de/person/424.
82 Franke (1984), 492; *Persons and Names of the Middle Kingdom*, Version 4 (person 424; accessed August 2, 2023) https://pnm.uni-mainz.de/person/492.
83 Olabarria (2020a), 102–103.
84 Olabarria (2020a), 115–204.
85 Olabarria (2020a), 42.
86 Simpson (1974), pl. 16; Olabarria (2020a), 267; Ilin-Tomich (2017), 103–104.
87 Franke (1984), no 401; *Persons and Names of the Middle Kingdom*, Version 4 (person 401; accessed August 2, 2023) https://pnm.uni-mainz.de/person/401.
88 Ward (1982), 212; Franke and Maree (2013), 19–21; see also *Persons and Names of the Middle Kingdom*, Version 4 (title 554; accessed August 2, 2023) https://pnm.uni-mainz.de/title/554.
89 Franke and Maree (2013), 20–21.
90 Simpson (1974), pl. 29; Wegner (2009), 103–105; Baligh (2008); Franke and Maree (2013), 42–42; Snape (2019), 266–270; Ilin-Tomich (2017), 78, 201; Twiston Davies and Nielsen (2019); Olabarria (2020a), 199, 208.
91 Ward (1982), 132; *Persons and Names of the Middle Kingdom*, Version 4 (title 132; accessed August 2, 2023) https://pnm.uni-mainz.de/title/132.

92 Franke (1984), 326; *Persons and Names of the Middle Kingdom*, Version 4 (person 326; accessed August 2, 2023) https://pnm.uni-mainz.de/ person/326.
93 Ward (1982), 1574; *Persons and Names of the Middle Kingdom*, Version 4 (title 1574; accessed August 2, 2023) https://pnm.uni-mainz.de/title/1574.
94 Franke (1984), 17; *Persons and Names of the Middle Kingdom*, Version 4 (person 17; accessed August 2, 2023) https://pnm.uni-mainz.de/ person/17.
95 Ward (1982), 574. *Persons and Names of the Middle Kingdom*, Version 4 (title 574; accessed August 2, 2023) https://pnm.uni-mainz.de/title/574.
96 Franke (1984), 350; *Persons and Names of the Middle Kingdom*, Version 4 (person 350; accessed August 2, 2023) https://pnm.uni-mainz.de/ person/350.
97 Ward (1982), 365; *Persons and Names of the Middle Kingdom*, Version 4 (title 365; accessed August 2, 2023) https://pnm.uni-mainz.de/title/365.
98 Franke (1984), 192; *Persons and Names of the Middle Kingdom*, Version 4 (person 350; accessed August 2, 2023) https://pnm.uni-mainz.de/ person/350.
99 Simpson (1974), 23; Wegner (2010); Snape (2019), 268–270; Olabarria (2020a), 199.
100 Simpson (1974), pl. 50; Ilin-Tomich (2017), 77; Olabarria (2020a), 210.
101 Ward (1982), 721; *Persons and Names of the Middle Kingdom*, Version 4 (title 721; accessed August 2, 2023) https://pnm.uni-mainz.de/title/721.
102 Franke (1984), 336; *Persons and Names of the Middle Kingdom*, Version 4 (person 336; accessed August 2, 2023) https://pnm.uni-mainz.de/ person/336.
103 Ward (1982), 347; *Persons and Names of the Middle Kingdom*, Version 4 (title 347; accessed August 2, 2023) https://pnm.uni-mainz.de/title/347.
104 Franke (1984), 447; *Persons and Names of the Middle Kingdom*, Version 4 (person 447; accessed August 2, 2023) https://pnm.uni-mainz.de/ person/447.
105 Ward (1982), 803; *Persons and Names of the Middle Kingdom*, Version 4 (title 803; accessed August 2, 2023) https://pnm.uni-mainz.de/title/803.
106 Franke (1984), 358; *Persons and Names of the Middle Kingdom*, Version 4 (person 358; accessed August 2, 2023) https://pnm.uni-mainz.de/ person/358; see also Franke and Marée (2013, 41–44).
107 Franke (1984), 325; *Persons and Names of the Middle Kingdom*, Version 4 (person 325; accessed August 2, 2023) https://pnm.uni-mainz.de/ person/325.
108 Stefanović (2016), 161.
109 See Prell (2012).
110 See Pagé-Perron (2018), 195 n. 5.
111 Watts and Strogatz (1998); Collar (2020), 49.
112 Granovetter (1973); Collar (2022), 4–14.
113 Depending on the assemblage of the data, nodes may range from individuals, to objects, to sites, regions, and countries. The same applies for the second element of networks, the links (ties) between nodes, which can be recognised as trade connections, family relationships, shared religious practice, material similarities, physical infrastructures such as roads, and so on. See Knappett (2011); Brughmans (2013); Collar (2020), 49; Brughmans and Peeples (2023).
114 Actor-Network Theory (ANT) developed in sociology as a non-anthropocentric "semiotics of materiality," which incorporates the active role of non-human aspects of society – objects, institutions, ideas, places, etc. – into relational networks of human and non-human participants. Within an ANT framework, humans and non-humans are locked into a hybrid, dispersed network through whose relations action emerges. Although ANT has come under heavy criticism for many reasons, it appears most suitable for the purpose of this paper and the analysed data. See Malafouris (2013), 123–149; Knappett (2005), 74–79; Collar (2020), 50; Van Oyen (2015); Knappett (2018); Knappett (2020).
115 Cliney (202x).

116 Knappett and Malafouris (2008).
117 Granovetter (1973); Collar (2022), 4–14.
118 Wetherell and Wellman (1996).
119 Knappett (2011); Brughmans (2013); Collar (2020), 50; Brughmans and Peeples (2023).
120 Collar (2020), 50.
121 See Costenbader and Valente (2003); Peeples et al. (2016).

References

Adams, M. D. (2010). The Stela of Nakht, son of Nemty: Contextualizing object and individual in the funerary landscape at Abydos. In Z. Hawass & J. H. Wegner (Eds.), *Millions of jubilees: Studies in honor of David P. Silverman* (pp. 1–25). Conseil Suprême des Antiquités de l'Égypte.

Andreu, G. (1980). La stèle Louvre C. 249: un complément à la reconstitution d'une chapelle abydénienne. *Bulletin de l'Institut français d'archéologie orientale, 80*, 139–147.

Baligh, R. (2008). Three Middle Kingdom Stelae from the Egyptian museum in Cairo. *Journal of the American Research Center in Egypt, 44*, 169–184.

Barabási, A.-L. (2003). *Linked: The new science of networks*. Perseus Publishing.

Berlev, O. D. (1976). Review of *The terrace of the great god at Abydos: The offering chapels of dynasties 12 and 13*. *Bibliotheca Orientalis, 33*(5/6), 324–326.

Berlev, O. D. (1987). A social experiment in Nubia during the years 9–17 of Sesostris I. In M. A. Powell (Ed.), *Labor in the ancient near east* (pp. 143–157). Eisenbrauns.

Bourdieu, P. (1983). Ökonomisches Kapital, kulturelles Kapital, soziales Kapital. *Soziale Welt, 2*, 183–198. https://doi.org/10.1007/978-3-531-18944-4_15

Brughmans, T. (2013). Thinking through networks: A review of formal network methods in archaeology. *Journal of Archaeological Method and Theory, 20*(4), 623–662. https://doi.org/10.1007/s10816-012-9133-8

Brughmans, T., & Peeples, M. (2017). Trends in archaeological network research: A bibliometric analysis. *Journal of Historical Network Research, 1*(1), 1–24. http://jhnr.uni.lu/index.php/jhnr/article/view/10

Brughmans, T., & Peeples, M. (2023). *Network science in archaeology*. Cambridge University Press. https://doi:10.1017/9781009170659

Budka, J. (2019). Re-awakening Osiris at Umm el-Qaab (Abydos): New evidence for Votive offerings and other religious practices. In N. Staring, H. Twiston Davies, & L. Weiss (Eds.), *Perspectives on lived religion: Practices – Transmission – Landscape* (pp. 15–25). Sidestone Press.

Cahail, K. (2022). Between town and temple. Exploring the influences of royal, religious and social institutions on funerary landscape at South Abydos during the new kingdom. In N. Staring, L. Weiss, & H. Twiston Davies (Eds.), *Perspectives on lived religion II: The making of a cultural geography* (pp. 125–138). Sidestone Press. https://doi.org/10.59641/e4i0177g

Chollier, V. (2019). Social network analysis in Egyptology: Benefits, methods and limits. *Journal of Egyptian Archaeology, 105*, 83–96. https://doi.org/10.1177/0307513319889329

Cliney, D. (202x). The social life of bronzes: Actor-network theory on the entangled acropolis. In N. Papalexandrou & A. S. Koch (Eds.), *Hephaestus on the acropolis. Selected papers on ancient art and architecture.* Retrieved August 8, 2023, from https://www.academia.edu/97884799/Proof_The_Social_Life_of_Bronzes_Actor_Network_Theory_on_the_Entangled_Acropolis

Collar, A. (2020). Networks, connectivity, and material culture. In C. Cooper (Ed.), *New approaches to ancient material culture in the Greek & Roman World. 21st-century methods and classical antiquity* (pp. 47–62). Brill. https://doi.org/10.1163/9789004440753_003

Collar, A. (2022). Strong ties, social networks, and the diffusion of new ideas. Who do you trust?. In A. Collar (Ed.), *Networks and the spread of ideas in the past strong ties, innovation and knowledge exchange* (pp. 1–27). Routledge. https://doi.org/10.4324/9780429429217

Cooney, J. (1974). Review of *The terrace of the great god at Abydos: The offering chapels of dynasties 12 and 13*. *American Journal of Archaeology*, 78(4), 433–434. https://doi.org/10.2307/502760

Costenbader, E., & Valente, T. W. (2003). The stability of centrality measures when networks are sampled. *Social Networks*, 25(4), 283–307. https://doi.org/10.1016/S0378-8733(03)00012-1

De Meulenaere, H. (1977). Review of *The terrace of the great god at Abydos: The offering chapels of dynasties 12 and 13*. *Chronique d'Égypte*, 52(103), 79–82. https://doi.org/10.1484/J.CDE.2.308428

DeVries, C. E. (1977). Review of *The terrace of the great god at Abydos: The offering chapels of dynasties 12 and 13*. *Journal of the American Oriental Society*, 97(4), 588–589. https://doi.org/10.2307/598661

El-Rabi'I, A.-M. (1977). Familles abydéniennes du Moyen Empire. *Chroniqued'Egypte*, 52(103), 13–21. https://doi.org/10.1484/J.CDE.2.308424

Effland, U., & Effland, A. (2013). *Abydos: Tor zur ägyptischen Unterwelt. Zaberns Bildbände zur Archäologie.* Philipp von Zabern.

Effland, U., Budka, J., & Effland, A. (2010). Studien zum Osiriskult in Umm el-Qaab/Abydos: ein Vorbericht. *Mitteilungen des Deutschen Archäologischen Instituts, Abteilung Kairo*, 66, 19–91.

Franke, D. (1983). *Altägyptische Verwandtschaftsbezeichnungen im Mittleren Reich.* Borg GMBH.

Franke, D. (1984). *Personendaten aus dem Mittleren Reich (20.–16. Jahrhundert v. Chr.): Dossiers 1–796.* Otto Harrassowitz.

Franke, D., & Marée, M. (2013). *Egyptian Stelae in the British Museum from the 13th–17th dynasties. Volume I, fascicule 1: Descriptions.* British Museum Press.

Freed, R. (1996). Stela workshops of early dynasty 12. In P. der Manuelian & R. Freed (Eds.), *Studies in honor of William Kelly Simpson* (pp. 297–336). Museum of Fine Arts.

Grajetzki, W. (2000). *Die höchsten Beamten der ägyptischen Zentralverwaltung zur Zeit des Mittleren Reiches. Prosopographie, Titel und Titelreihen.* Achet.

Grajetzki, W. (2001). *Two treasurers of the late Middle Kingdom.* Archaeopress.

Grajetzki, W. (2009). *Court officials of the Egyptian Middle Kingdom.* Bloomsbury Publishing.

Grajetzki, W. (2013). Setting a state anew: The central administration from the end of the Old Kingdom to the end of the Middle Kingdom. In J. C. Moreno García

(Ed.), *Ancient Egyptian administration* (pp. 215–258). Brill. https://doi.org/10.1163
/9789004250086_009
Grajetzki, W., & Stefanović, D. (2012). *Dossiers of Ancient Egyptians – The Middle Kingdom and second intermediate period: Addition to Franke's "Personendaten."* Golden House Publications.
Granovetter, M. (1973). The strength of weak ties. *American Journal of Sociology*, *78*(6), 1360–1380. http://www.jstor.org/stable/2776392
Herzberg, A. (2019). Prosopographia Memphitica – Analyzing prosopographical data and personal networks from the Memphite necropolis. In N. Staring, H. Twiston Davies, & L. Weiss (Eds.), *Perspectives on lived religion: Practices – Transmission – Landscape* (pp. 39–58). Sidestone Press.
Herzberg-Beiersdorf, A. (2023). *Prosopographia Memphitica. Individuelle Identitäten und kollektive Biographien einer königlichen Residenzstadt des Neuen Reichs.* De Gruyter. https://doi.org/10.1515/9783110783650
Ilin-Tomich, A. (2014). Review of 'Dossiers of ancient Egyptians – the Middle Kingdom and second intermediate period: Addition to Franke's "Personendaten". *Bibliotheca Orientalis*, *71*(1–2), 136–146.
Ilin-Tomich, A. (2017). *From workshop to sanctuary: The production of late Middle Kingdom memorial stelae.* Golden House Publications.
Ilin-Tomich, A. (2023). Aufwärter der Bier- und Brotkammer Sa-ii und Eje, ihre Verwandtschaft und Berufsstand. In S. Gerhards, N. Gräßler, S. A. Gülden, A. Ilin-Tomich, J. Kertmann, A. Kilian, T. Konrad, K. van der Moezel, & M. Zöller-Engelhardt (Eds.), *Schöne Denkmäler sind entstanden: Studien zu Ehren von Ursula Verhoeven* (pp. 179–199). https://doi.org/10.11588/propylaeum.1085.c16601
Knappett, C. (2005). *Thinking through material culture: An interdisciplinary perspective. Archaeology, culture, and society.* University of Pennsylvania Press. http://www.jstor.org/stable/j.ctt3fhh6q
Knappett, C. (2011). *An archaeology of interaction: Network perspectives on material culture and society.* Oxford University Press. https://doi.org/10.1093/acprof:osobl /9780199215454.001.0001
Knappett, C. (2018). From network connectivity to human mobility: Models for minoanization. *Journal of Archaeological Method and Theory*, *25*, 974–995. https://doi.org/10.1007/s10816-018-9396-9
Knappett, C. (2020). Relational concepts and challenges to network analysis in social archaeology. In L. Donnellan (Ed.), *Archaeological networks and social interaction* (pp. 20–37). Routledge. https://doi.org/10.4324/9781351003063
Knappett, C., & Malafouris, L. (2008). Material and nonhuman agency: An introduction. In C. Knappett & L. Malafouris (Eds.), *Material agency: Towards a non-anthropocentric approach* (pp. ix–xix). Springer.
Kopleff, H. J. (2017). *A community in stone: The 'Cenotaph' Stelae of Abydos* [Unpublished doctoral dissertation]. New York University.
Kucharek, A. (2006). Die Prozession des Osiris in Abydos: zur Signifikanz archäologischer Quellen für die Rekonstruktion eines zentralen Festrituals. In J. Mylonopoulos & H. Roeder (Eds.), *Archäologie und Ritual: auf der Suche nach der rituellen Handlung in den antiken Kulturen Ägyptens und Griechenlands* (pp. 53–64). Phoibos.
Landgráfová, R. (2011). *It is my good name that you should remember: Egyptian biographical texts on Middle Kingdom stelae.* Czech Institute of Egyptology.

Landvatter, T. (2021). Review of *Kinship and family in ancient Egypt: Archaeology and anthropology in dialogue*. *African Archaeological Review*, *38*(3), 547–549. https://doi.org/10.1007/s10437-021-09438-6

Leahy, A. (1989). A protective measure at Abydos in the thirteenth dynasty. *Journal of Egyptian Archaeology*, *75*, 41–60. https://doi.org/10.1177/030751338907500105

Leprohon, R. J. (2019). Self-presentation in the twelfth dynasty. In H. Bassir (Ed.), *Living forever: Self-presentation in ancient Egypt* (pp. 105–123). American University in Cairo Press.

Lichtheim, M. (1988). *Ancient Egyptian autobiographies chiefly of the Middle Kingdom: A study and an anthology*. Vandenhoeck & Ruprecht GmbH KG.

Malafouris, L. (2013). *How things shape the mind: A theory of material engagement*. The MIT Press. https://doi.org/10.7551/mitpress/9476.001.0001

Marée, M. (2010). A sculpture workshop at Abydos from the late Sixteenth or early Seventeenth Dynasty. In M. Marée (Ed.), *The second intermediate period (Thirteenth-Seventeenth Dynasties): Current research, future prospects* (pp. 241–281). Peeters Publishers.

Mills, B. (2017). Social network analysis in archaeology. *Annual Review of Anthropology*, *46*, 379–397. https://doi.org/10.1146/annurev-anthro-102116-041423

Moreno García, J. C. (2013). The 'other' administration. Patronage, factions, and informal networks of power in ancient Egypt. In J. C. Moreno García (Ed.), *Ancient Egyptian administration* (pp. 1029–1065). Brill. https://doi.org/10.1163/9789004250086_023

Moreno García, J. C. (2020). Clientele, power and family bonds in Ancient Egypt: Building social links, promoting individual strategies, facing kin conflicts. *Soziale Systeme*, *25*(1), 30–60. https://doi.org/10.1515/sosys-2020-0002

Newman, M. (2010). *Networks: An introduction*. Oxford University Press. https://doi.org/10.1093/acprof:oso/9780199206650.001.0001

O'Connor, D. (1985). The "cenotaphs" of the Middle Kingdom at Abydos'. In P. Posener-Kriéger (Ed.), *Mélanges Gamal Eddin Mokhtar* (pp. 161–177). Institut Français d'Archéologie Orientale du Caire.

O'Connor, D. (2009). *Abydos: Egypt's first pharaohs and the cult of Osiris*. Thames & Hudson.

Olabarria, L. (2014). *Materialising kinship, constructing relatedness: Kin group display and commemoration in First Intermediate Period and Middle Kingdom Egypt (ca 2150–1650 BCE). Volume one: Text and biography* [Unpublished doctoral dissertation]. University of Oxford.

Olabarria, L. (2020a). *Kinship and family in ancient Egypt. Archaeology and anthropology in dialogue*. Cambridge University Press. https://doi.org/10.1017/9781108670487

Olabarria, L. (2020b). Coming to terms with stelae: A performative approach to memorial Stelae and chapels of Abydos in the Middle Kingdom. *Studien zur Altägyptischen Kultur*, *49*, 118–178.

Oppenheim, A. (2015). Artists and workshops: The complexity of creation. In A. Oppenheim, D. Arnold, D. Arnold, & K. Yamamoto (Eds.), *Ancient Egypt transformed: The Middle Kingdom* (pp. 23–27). The Metropolitan Museum of Art.

Oppenheim, A., Arnold, D., Arnold, D., & Yamamoto, K. (Eds.). (2015). *Ancient Egypt transformed: The Middle Kingdom*. The Metropolitan Museum of Art.

Pagé-Perron, É. (2018). Network analysis for reproducible research on large administrative cuneiform corpora. In B. Juloux, A. R. Gansell, & A. Di Ludovico (Eds.), *Cyber research on the ancient near east and neighboring regions: Case studies on archaeological data, objects, texts, and digital archiving* (pp. 194–223). Brill. https://doi.org/10.1163/9789004375086_008

Pálsson, G. (2020). Cutting the network, knotting the line: A linaeological approach to network analysis. *Journal of Archaeological Method and Theory, 28*, 178–196. https://doi.org/10.1007/s10816-020-09450-1

Peeples, M. A. Mills, B. J. Haas, W. R. J. Clark, J. J. & Roberts, J. M. J. (2016). Analytical challenges for the application of social network analysis in archaeology. In T. Brughmans, A. Collar, & F. Coward (Eds.), *The connected past: Challenges to network studies in archaeology and history* (pp. 59–84). Oxford University Press. https://doi.org/10.1093/9780198748519.003.0010

Pillon, A. (2022). La terrasse d'Hathor à Dendara et la réversion des offrandes divines: un élément du paysagecultuel des villes au Moyen Empire. *Bulletin de l'Institut français d'archéologie orientale, 122*, 451–491. https://doi.org/10.4000/bifao.12269

Prell, C. (2012). *Social network analysis: History, theory and methodology*. Sage Publications.

Quirke, S. (1990). *The administration of Egypt in the late Middle Kingdom: The hieratic documents*. SIA Publications.

Quirke, S. (2004). *Titles and bureaux of Egypt, 1850–1700 BC*. Golden House Publications.

Regulski, I. (Ed.). (2019). *Abydos: The sacred land at the western horizon*. Peeters Publishers. https://doi.org/10.2307/j.ctv1q26pqk

Revez, J. (2003). The metaphorical use of the kinship term sn "brother". *Journal of the American Research Center in Egypt, 40*, 123–131. https://doi.org/10.2307/40000295

Roccati, A. (2003). Quattro stele del Medio Regno. In S. Quirke (Ed.), *Discovering Egypt from the Neva: The Egyptological legacy of Oleg D. Berlev* (pp. 111–121). Achet Verlag.

Rosell, P. M. (2021). A new family to the ANOC groups: A study of Stelae CG 20077 and CG 20098. *Journal of Egyptian History, 14*(2), 203–228. https://doi.org/10.1163/18741665-bja10008

Scott, J., & Carrington, P. J. (Eds.). (2011). *The SAGE handbook of social network analysis*. SAGE Publishing.

Silverman, D. P. (1977). Review of *The terrace of the great god at Abydos: The offering chapels of dynasties 12 and 13*. *Journal of Near Eastern Studies, 36*(3), 221–222. https://doi.org/10.1086/372570

Simpson, W. K. (1974). *The terrace of the great god at Abydos: The offering chapels of dynasties 12 and 13*. Peabody Museum of Natural History of Yale University & University of Pennsylvania Museum of Archaeology and Anthropology.

Simpson, W. K., Ritner, R. K., Tobin, V. A., & Wente, E. F. (Eds.). (2003). *The literature of ancient Egypt: An anthology of stories, instructions, and poetry*. Yale University Press. http://www.jstor.org/stable/j.ctt5vm2m5

Smith, M. (2017). *Following Osiris: Perspectives on the Osirian afterlife from four millennia*. Oxford University Press. https://doi.org/10.1093/acprof:oso/9780199582228.001.0001

Snape, S. (2011). *Ancient Egyptian tombs: The cultures of life and death.* Wiley-Blackwell.

Snape, S. (2019). Memorial monuments at Abydos and the "Terrace of the Great God". In I. Regulski (Ed.), *Abydos: The sacred land at the western horizon* (pp. 255–272). Peeters Publishers. http://www.jstor.org/stable/j.ctv1q26pqk.17

Spaull, C. H. (1975). Review of *The terrace of the great god at Abydos: The offering chapels of dynasties 12 and 13. Journal of Egyptian Archaeology, 65,* 283–284. https://doi.org/10.1177/030751337506100152

Stefanović, D. (2016). *Dossiers of ancient Egyptian women: The Middle Kingdom and second intermediate period.* Golden House Publications.

Stefanović, D. (2019a). The social network(s) of the Middle Kingdom and second intermediate period treasurers: Rehuerdjersen, Siese, Ikhernefret and Senebsumai. *Journal of Egyptian History, 12*(2), 259–287. https://doi.org/10.1163/18741665-12340054

Stefanović, D. (2019b). Varia Epigraphica VI: The Middle Kingdom. *Göttinger Miszellen. Beiträge zur ägyptologischen Diskussion, 257,* 177–185.

Stefanović, D. (2020). *From ego-network to the global network – The world of the Middle Kingdom treasurer Senebi.* https://www.youtube.com/watch?v=JVWiegO76yY

Twiston Davies, H., & Nielsen, N. (2019). Garstang Stela E.31 and the family of Iy at Abydos. *Zeitschrift für Ägyptische Sprache und Altertumskunde, 146*(1), 69–81. https://doi.org/10.1515/zaes-2019-0009

Van Oyen, A. (2015). Actor-network theory's take on archaeological types: Becoming, material agency and historical explanation. *Cambridge Archaeological Journal, 25*(1), 63–78. https://doi.org/10.1017/S0959774314000705

Végh, Z. (2019). The mʿḥʿ.t of Osiris in Asyut. In I. Regulski (Ed.), *Abydos: The sacred land at the western horizon* (pp. 301–313). Peeters Publishers. https://doi.org/10.2307/j.ctv1q26pqk.19

Volokhine, Y. (1998). Les déplacements pieuxs en Égypte pharaonique: sites et practiques cultuelles. In D. Frankfurter (Ed.), *Pilgrimage and holy space in late antique Egypt* (pp. 51–97). Brill. https://doi.org/10.1163/9789004298064_003

Ward, W. A. (1982). *Index of Egyptian administrative and religious titles of the Middle Kingdom: With a glossary of words and phrases used.* American University of Beirut.

Wasserman, S., & Faust, K. (1994). *Social network analysis: Methods and applications.* Cambridge University Press. https://doi.org/10.1017/CBO9780511815478

Watts, D. J., & Strogatz, S. H. (1998). Collective dynamics of "Small-World" networks. *Nature, 393*(6684), 440–442. https://doi:10.1038/30918

Wegner, J. (1996). *The mortuary complex of Senwosret III: A study of Middle Kingdom state activity and the cult of Osiris at Abydos* [Unpublished doctoral dissertation]. University of Pennsylvania.

Wegner, J. (2001). The town of Wah-sut at South Abydos: 1999 excavations. *Mitteilungen des Deutschen Archäologischen Instituts, Abteilung Kairo, 57,* 281–308.

Wegner, J. (2009). The tomb of Senwosret III at Abydos: Considerations on the origins and development of the Royal Amduat tomb. In D. Silverman, W. K. Simpson, & J. Wegner (Eds.), *Archaism and innovation: Studies in the culture of Middle Kingdom Egypt* (pp. 103–169). Yale Egyptological Seminar.

Wegner, J. (2010). External connections of the community Wah-Sut during the late Middle Kingdom. In P. der Manuelian & R. B. Hussein (Eds.), *Perspectives on ancient Egypt: Studies in honor of Edward Brovarski* (pp. 437–458). Conseil Suprême des Antiquités de l'Égypte.

Wegner, J. (2015). Abydos. In A. Oppenheim, D. Arnold, D. Arnold, & K. Yamamoto (Eds.), *Ancient Egypt transformed: The Middle Kingdom* (pp. 317–318). The Metropolitan Museum of Art.

Wegner, J., Cahail, K., Hill, J., Rosado, M., & Gleeson, M. (2021). *King Seneb-Kay's tomb and the necropolis of a lost dynasty at Abydos*. University of Pennsylvania Press. https://doi.org/10.2307/j.ctv19fvzx2

Wellman, B., & Wetherell, C. (1996). Social network analysis of historical communities: Some questions from the present for the past. *History of the Family*, *1*(1), 97–121. https://doi.org/10.1016/S1081-602X(96)90022-6

Yamamoto, K. (2009). *A Middle Kingdom pottery assemblage from North Abydos* [Unpublished doctoral dissertation]. University of Toronto.

Yamamoto, K. (2015). Abydos and Osiris: The terrace of the great god. In A. Oppenheim, D. Arnold, D. Arnold, & K. Yamamoto (Eds.), *Ancient Egypt transformed: The Middle Kingdom* (pp. 250–252). The Metropolitan Museum of Art.

6 Some final remarks for future research

Giovani Ruffini states, in the concluding chapter of the volume *The ties that bind: Ancient politics and network research*, that his overview "ends with a methodological note on network analytical best practices, coupled with a healthy dose of skepticism: network analysis is a useful tool for the analysis of antiquity, but perhaps not in the way we have thought it is."[1] Indeed, network theory is, from its very beginning, heterogeneous, without strict theoretical and methodological unity, and is not created either for historical or archaeological research. Theoretically, this approach is far from that of Egyptology. The same applies for all network analysis subbranches, including Social Network Analysis, as I have briefly outlined on the previous pages.

One of the main obstacles for all historical and archaeological disciplines, including Egyptology, when we consider the network approach, is incomplete datasets. Our own perception of sources, or segments of the past we are trying to reconstruct, or toward questions we are inclined to answer inevitably results in the subjective selection of data we are dealing with. As Ruffini points out, "one author, given the data of another, might readily arrive at a different network and thus at different conclusions. This variability poses a real problem for historical network analysis as a scientific project. It renders almost impossible the verifiability necessary for any scientific experiment."[2] Indeed, the same may apply for any other methodology used, either by an archaeologist or historian – or, in our case, an Egyptologist.

Setting aside rather complex epistemological and tautological questions, or issues of agency, completeness of modelled social structures, temporality, validity of measurements for incomplete networks, and chosen criteria for selection of data, visualisation is one of the greatest advantages of Social Network Analysis for any Egyptologist interested in social history and prosopography. To be able to 'see' at once, for example, a network of an extended household (like one belonging to Sneferu, briefly outlined in Chapter 4),[3] or of a rather complex community (as is exemplified by documents from Ptolemaic Pathyris),[4] instead of losing sight within complex genealogical charts, which very often may have missed some links because we cannot detect from the sources how to transfer rather complicated kin terms into charts, is an indisputable advantage. Indeed, results from time to time may be modest, but sometimes the software may recognise 'a bridge' – in many cases 'a female' link – connecting otherwise distant and (supposedly) unrelated groups, which, in a longer run may shed new light on certain aspects of relatedness with the analysed community.

What can be seen in the graph? All of our modelled networks are, as stressed repeatedly, fragmented and consequently reflect a distorted snapshot of past reality. Therefore, it may look as if we are fighting a lost battle from the very beginning. Network theory and Social Network Analysis were created to study an actual social structure. This is not the case in either Egyptology or any other historical or archaeological discipline. Sociologists carefully choose a sample group or a representative body of subjects they want to analyse and address questions. We cannot do that. The sources available to us are of great limitation – typology of preserved data (tomb inscriptions, stelae, ostraca etc.), the context and purpose of object production – funerary or non-funerary, patterns of representations of individuals on objects – kin groups, collegial groups or something else,[5] or something rather prosaic but equally important – the level of preservation.

Although these limitations may produce a graph that reflects a distorted image of social (or any other) reality, the same applies to any other chosen methodological approach in both history and archaeology.[6] Our networks are blurred and fragmented modelled images of reality, but the actors and actants who created them are stable components. A king or high-ranking dignitary will be a node with the highest degree within the network without any doubt, although the betweenness centrality may vary with the addition or removal of actors from a network. We also need to keep in mind that any modelled network (regardless of who the actors are and what type of relatedness we are trying to analyse) was certainly denser than that reflected in the preserved sources. We do not know how many objects, for example, any of the considered individuals, have had, or have been attested on it, and how many additional individuals were part of their networks.

However, the network approach, Social Network Analysis and Actor-Network Theory may help us to test our results. Even if the modelled network has a structure that confirms the previously achieved results, its implementation would be worthwhile.

Ruffini points out that he "continue(s) to believe that network analysis is a useful methodology for the study of the ancient world," but also stresses that this is not "simply a matter of entering the data into the computer and analyzing the results that come out the other end, imagining that they represent the social reality of the ancient world. Rather, network analysis is likely to become only the first step in a longer and more complicated process. It does let us measure the shape of the surviving evidence, to gain a "God's eye view" of all of the surviving social connections. But then we must go a step further, and form and test hypotheses about what factors distort this evidence, what changes in the fabric of ancient society as it is squeezed into the mould of the written word to meet the circumstances of any given corner of the written world. And then, in turn, we must duplicate and re-test these hypotheses as they are put forward by others, in a truly iterative and scientific collaboration."[7]

The same applies to Egyptology as well. Although the modelled networks presented in Chapter 5 certainly require further development to confirm their validity, the author believes that they represent an acceptable starting point for Egyptologists interested in social history and historical and archaeological networks. The presented case-studies further address the potential of using network analysis in research, both diachronically and spatially, on complex datasets. As with any other methodological approach, we do not always have a definite answer or a final conclusion but a stimulating and challenging tool for testing our hypotheses and assumptions. This also applies to the results presented in this book: they are perhaps more interesting if considered as a first step towards future comparative studies involving other microhistories, administrative offices, or sites. It would be worth comparing the networks of Late Middle Kingdom viziers, or other high-ranking officials, to see whether they reflect the same patterns of relatedness as outlined by networks of treasurers.

Future research on Abydos memorial chapels (ANOC) hopefully will strengthen the idea that the 'votive zone' should be considered as, to use the words of Jeanette Kopleff, "a community in stone."[8] Indeed, chapels were connected through people mentioned on the objects belonging to them. The material from Lahun, Wah-Sut, Deir el Medina, and Amarna are also worthy of research.

With all limitations and obstacles that any Egyptologist will face with Social Network Analysis and Actor-Network Theory approach, the words of George Kubler from *The Shape of Time* may be worth of having in mind: "every trait of a thing is both a cluster of subordinate traits as well as subordinate part of another cluster."[9]

Notes

1 Ruffini (2020), 326.
2 Ruffini (2020), 335.
3 See Figure 4.1.
4 Tambs (2022).
5 Olabarria (2022).
6 See also Chollier (2019).
7 Ruffini (2020), 338.
8 Kopleff (2017).
9 Kubler (1962), 36.

References

Chollier, V. (2019). Social network analysis in Egyptology: Benefits, methods and limits. *Journal of Egyptian Archaeology*, *105*, 83–96. https://doi.org/10.1177/0307513319889329

Kopleff, H. J. (2017). *A community in stone: The 'Cenotaph' Stelae of Abydos* [Unpublished doctoral dissertation]. New York University.

Kubler, G. (1962). *The shape of time: Remarks on the history of things*. Yale University Press. https://www.jstor.org/stable/j.ctt5vkx7n

Olabarria, L. (2022). The power of convention: Reinterpreting social groups through a Middle Kingdom statuette. *Journal of Egyptian Archaeology*, *108*, 143–157. https://doi.org/10.1177/03075133221141909

Ruffini, G. R. (2020). An epilogue. Social network analysis and Greco-Roman politics. *Journal of Historical Network Research*, *4*, 325–339. https://doi.org/10.25517/jhnr.v4i0.82

Tambs, L. (2022). *Socio-economic relations in Ptolemaic Pathyris: A network analytical approach to a bilingual community*. Brill. https://doi.org/10.1163/9789004500266

Index

Abydos 4, 49–56, 66–71, 73–5, 78n1, 92
Abydos North Offering Chapel (ANOC) 52–8, 61–3, 68–74, 77, 92
Actor-Network Theory (ANT) 4, 15, 17n35, 73, 78, 82n114, 91–2
administration 25, 40, 55, 65–6, 71
Akkad 4
Alexander, M. 2, 15
Amarna 22–3, 25, 34, 92
Amenemhet III 55
Ancient Near Eastern Studies 1–4, 23, 33, 35, 43
Ansell, C. 2
Aphrodito 2, 20–1
archive *see* Amarna; cuneiform texts; Kaneš; Lahun
Asiatics 40–1
Aššur 4, 34
Assyria 4, 34
Assyriology 3–4, 24, 27

betweenness centrality *see* network measurements
bipartite *see* network types
Bourdieu, P. 13
Bridge: concept of 12–14, 57, 72–3, 91
Broux, Y. 26
Brughmans, T. 3–4

centralisation *see* network measurements
chapel *see* ANOC
Chollier, V. 24, 33, 35, 37–48

classical studies 1–4, 27, 33, 35, 43
Cline, D. H. 22–3
closeness *see* network measurements
Collar, A. 3, 15, 76
complex network *see* network types
Connected Past group 2–3
Coward, F. 3
cuneiform texts 22–3

Danowski, J. 2, 15
degree *see* network measurements
Deir el Medina 34, 40, 45n33, 92
Dekker, R. 21–2
density *see* network measurements
Depauw, M. 23
Dogaer, N. 23
Dulíková, V. 25, 33, 40, 42
Dutrey, C. 24
dynamic network *see* network types

edge *see* network elements
ego-network *see* network types
Egypt, periodisation: Byzantine 2, 20–2, 26; Coptic 50; Early dynastic 4, 50–1; Graeco-Roman 26; Middle Kingdom 4–5, 25, 34, 38, 40–2, 50–2, 55, 61, 64, 67, 74, 76, 92; New Kingdom 22, 24; Old Kingdom 25, 42, 51; Ptolemaic 22–3, 26, 90; Second Intermediate Period 25, 40
Egypt, sites *see* Abydos; Amarna; Aphrodito; Deir el Medina; Lahun; Memphis; Oxyrhynchos; Pathyris
El-Rabi'I, A.-M. 53, 61

Fitzenreiter, M. 25
Franke, D. 59

Göbekli Tepe 77
Graham, S. 2
Granovetter, M. 8, 13
graph theory 1, 5, 10, 13–14, 37, 72, 75

Herzberg-Beiersdorf, A. 24, 40, 54
Historical Network Research Community 3, 27
household 34–5, 37, 40, 43, 54, 56, 66, 69, 90
humanities 1, 21, 24

Ikhernefret 25, 55–60
Ilin-Tomich, A. 62, 79n38

Kaneš 4, 34
kin group 12, 54–5, 69–70, 91
Knappett, C. 27
koinography 70

Lahun 34–5, 92
Latour, B. 15, 17n35

macro network *see* network types
Mařík, R. 25, 40, 42
Martinet, É. 25, 33, 40–1
Memphis 24–5, 54, 67
micro network *see* network types
Milgram, S. 8
modularity *see* network measurements
monopartite *see* network types
Moreno, J. 8
multiplexity *see* network measurements

Nebankh 65, 67–9
necropolis *see* Abydos; Memphis
network elements: edge 9–11, 35, 56–7, 63, 69, 72–3, 80n47, 82n113; node 9–14, 16n10, 21, 35, 38, 56–7, 63, 68, 72–3, 80n47, 82n113, 91
network measurements: betweenness centrality 12, 13, 69, 91; centralisation 11, 13; closeness 12–13, 37; degree 10–11, 13, 57, 69, 75, 91; density 2, 10–11, 57; modularity 13; multiplexity 11; symmetry 11, 15, 73
network theory 2–4, 9, 22, 27, 33–4, 37, 41, 43, 75, 90–1
network types: bipartite 10, 14, 57, 72; complex network 9, 24–5, 41, 63; dynamic network 10–11, 35; ego-network 9, 12–13, 38, 43, 56–7, 61, 65, 72–3; macro network 10, 15, 57–8, 61, 74–5; micro network 10, 15, 34, 39–40, 43, 61; monopartite 10, 57, 72; one-mode 10, 56, 61–2, 72–3, 80n47; two-mode 10, 21, 26–7, 57, 61–2, 72–3, 80n47
node *see* network elements

office 38, 40, 55, 64, 68, 80n42
Olabarria, L. 53–5, 69–70
one-mode network *see* network types
Osiris 50–2, 55–6, 66, 68–71, 78n7, 78n11
Oxyrhynchos 2, 20–1

Padgett, J. F. 2
Pagé-Perron, É. 4
Papyrus Brooklyn 35.1446 40–1
Persons and Names of the Middle Kingdom (PNM) 5, 38
prosopography 20, 23, 25–6, 37–9, 41, 44n18, 54, 61, 69, 77, 90

Rehuankh 65, 68–9
Réseaux et Histoire 3
Rollinger, C. 35, 37
Ruffini, G. 2, 20–2, 39, 90–1

Sacco, A. 25
Šalim-Aššur 35
Senebi 58, 61–9, 74–5
Senebsumai 25, 58, 61–2, 64, 69
Senen 65
Senusret III 55–6
Sicard, C. 50

Simpson, W. K. 52–3
small world: concept of 4, 13–14,
  23, 34, 69, 73
Sneferu 34–5, 90
snowball method 9, 38
social capital 12–13, 16n23, 54, 79n30
sociogram 8, 10, 37, 75
software package 4–5, 10, 13–14,
  16n10, 21–3, 35, 38, 57, 75, 90
symmetry *see* network measurements

Tambs, L. 22–3, 33, 40
Teigen, H. F. 23
Terrace of the Great God 52–3
title 38, 40, 54–5, 58–9, 64, 69–72,
  75, 80n42
treasurer 25, 55–8, 61–9, 71, 74–5,
  80n42, 92

Trismegistos 26–7, 28n44
two-mode network *see* network
  types

Umm el Qa'āb 51–2

visualisation 8, 14, 23, 35, 38, 41,
  43, 72, 77, 90

Waerzeggers, C. 3
Wah-Sut 50, 71, 92
Wegner, J. 51–2
Wellman, B. 20, 74
Wetherell, C. 20, 74
workshop 2–3, 9, 14, 25, 53–4, 61,
  69–71, 78n9, 79n13

Zell, M. 15

For Product Safety Concerns and Information please contact our EU representative GPSR@taylorandfrancis.com
Taylor & Francis Verlag GmbH, Kaufingerstraße 24, 80331 München, Germany

www.ingramcontent.com/pod-product-compliance
Lightning Source LLC
Chambersburg PA
CBHW051758230426
43670CB00012B/2341